VIEWPOINT DIVERSITY

WHAT IT IS, WHY WE NEED IT, AND HOW TO GET IT

EDITED BY

John Tomasi & Bernard Schweizer

Heresy Press books may be purchased in bulk at special discounts for sales promotion, corporate gifts, fund-raising, or educational purposes. Special editions can also be created to specifications. For details, contact the Special Sales Department, Heresy Press, 307 Fifth Avenue, 4th Floor, New York, NY 10016 or info@skyhorsepublishing.com.

Visit our website at skyhorsepublishing.com.

HERESY PRESS LLC
P.O. Box 425201
Cambridge, MA 02142
heresy-press.com

10 9 8 7 6 5 4 3 2

Library of Congress Cataloging-in-Publication Data is available on file.

Cover design by Janelle Delia

Print ISBN: 978-1-949846-91-1
Ebook ISBN: 978-1-949846-92-8

Printed in the United States of America

Praise for *Viewpoint Diversity*

"As a vocal proponent of viewpoint diversity in higher education and elsewhere, I find this collection to be both bracing and necessary. *Viewpoint Diversity*, edited by Tomasi and Schweizer, offers compelling arguments to combat ideological homogeneity. From Yascha Mounk to Nadine Strossen, from Danielle Allen to Tyler VanderWeele, the contributors demonstrate that viewpoint diversity is much more than a loaded buzzword, positioning it as a vital ingredient in the pursuit of truth and the enrichment of our collective human experience."

—Steven Pinker, author of *When Everyone Knows That Everyone Knows . . . Common Knowledge and the Mysteries of Money, Power, and Everyday Life*

"*Viewpoint Diversity* is the handbook we've been missing: rigorous without being preachy, pluralistic without being naïve, and unapologetically pro–free speech. It makes the case—patiently and persuasively—that intellectual humility isn't a vibe; it's a practice, and institutions need rules and norms that reward truth-seeking instead of tribal applause. If you're tired of outrage-as-a-personality and ready to trade reflexes for curiosity, this book lays out a real path back to open inquiry—and a liberal democracy that can handle disagreement again."

—Greg Lukianoff, President of FIRE and coauthor of *The War On Words: 10 Arguments Against Free Speech—And Why They Fail*

"The term viewpoint diversity gets thrown around so often lately that it's easy to forget its literal meaning. Rather than shorthand for an exasperation with weaponized wokeness, it's actually a long intellectual journey in an often uncomfortable seat. This volume, edited by two of our most committed free speech champions and bringing together many of today's sharpest thinkers, is essential reading for the trip. I appreciated all of it and didn't agree with some of it, which is precisely the point."

—Meghan Daum, author of *The Catastrophe Hour: Selected Essays*

"Is viewpoint diversity a chimera? A conservative plot? Is it even really a thing? The all-star authors of this important collection put flesh on the concept and grapple with the opportunities and challenges it poses. Together, they show that viewpoint diversity—properly understood, sensibly implemented—offers a path to better teaching, sounder science, and a less polarized society."

—Jonathan Rauch, author of *Cross Purposes: Christianity's Broken Bargain with Democracy*

"This book on viewpoint diversity is what we need—a discussion on why this is so important to our democracy, our universities, and our society. What I like most about this book is that it promotes the very nature of pluralism—the various articles written by thought leaders show viewpoint diversity and that the reasons for it are indeed varied. This is a must read for anyone interested in open inquiry and pluralism."

—Jeremy Haefner, Chancellor of the University of Denver

"What is viewpoint diversity? Why does it matter? What are its limits? John Tomasi and Bernard Schweizer have convened an excellent array of thought leaders and essays to work through these questions. The book is a great primer for helping stakeholders understand the meaning and value of this much-contested concept, and it's a fantastic resource for those interested in reforming and improving institutions of knowledge and cultural production."

—Musa al-Gharbi, author of *We Have Never Been Woke: The Cultural Contradictions of a New Elite*

"The liberal culture that cherishes viewpoint diversity is today severely challenged. We need to think about this problem creatively and capaciously—this collection of first-rate authors points the way."

—Jenna Silber Storey, Co-Director of the Center for the Future of the American University, American Enterprise Institute

"We must all be grateful for this volume. Freedom of speech is the lifeblood of any college or university worth its name, but it is a pathetic and anemic institution that satisfies itself with free speech unless it is joined to a true marketplace of ideas enabled by viewpoint diversity. These essays illuminate that landscape."

—Michael Poliakoff, President of the American Council of Trustees and Alumni

Contents

Preface

by Jonathan Haidt

When I was a young man, I was very opinionated and confident in my opinions. On matters of politics and policy I was especially insufferable. But then I set out to write a book on the psychology of morality and politics, which became *The Righteous Mind.* I wanted to understand progressives, conservatives, and libertarians in their own terms, so I read their best writings and listened to their smartest thinkers. And then, something amazing happened. I discovered that there really are multiple internally coherent perspectives on complex social questions, and that each one gave me answers to questions I hadn't even known to ask.

I had discovered the wisdom of John Stuart Mill. I would not read him for another five years, as I was co-founding Heterodox Academy, but by trying on multiple perspectives I came to grasp Mill's famous line that "he who knows only his own side of the case knows little of that." Some readers of this volume will know the widely quoted next sentence of that passage, about how if you don't even know what the other side's reasons are, then you have no reason to believe that your side is right. But fewer will know the sentence after that, which is less widely quoted:

> Nor is it enough that he should hear the opinions of adversaries from his own teachers, presented as they state them, and accompanied by what they offer as refutations.

> He must be able to hear them from persons who actually believe them . . . he must know them in their most plausible and persuasive form.

It is this passage that best shows us the value of viewpoint diversity on campus and in course syllabi. Humans are highly social creatures who need to grasp ideas intuitively before we can process evidence and arguments about their truth. Therefore, talking face to face, or in a small group, has a special power to open minds and build new mental structures. Western philosophy began that way, with people in dialogue, and that's what a college education does well, when it includes enough viewpoint diversity.

That's why this book is so important: It's the first comprehensive book on viewpoint diversity in higher education, politics, and the arts. The editors have assembled an all-star cast of well-known professors and journalists. They all agree that viewpoint diversity is valuable, but because they come from different fields and different political starting points (left, right, center, and libertarian) they'll give you a variety of ways to think about this powerful yet understudied form of diversity.

At a time when liberal democracies are facing new challenges from the fragmenting effects of social media and AI, a book on how we benefit from interacting with each other across lines of difference could not be more timely.

Introduction

by the Editors

This volume is an urgent exploration of the importance of viewpoint diversity across various areas—particularly in higher education, political culture, and in the literary world. In our polarized political climate, viewpoint diversity has become a political football, with partisans on the right championing the concept as an antidote to conformity while partisans on the left denounce it as a "Trojan horse" or MAGA plot to fill the university with more Republicans. By contrast, this book presents a series of nuanced and intellectually rigorous investigations into the concept of viewpoint diversity. Our authors offer serious explorations of what it is and multiple ways of understanding its utility, while also facing the challenges of how best to implement viewpoint diversity in the real world. Collectively, the essays call for a renewed commitment to the core values of free speech, intellectual humility, and societal pluralism.

Part I: Viewpoint Diversity in Higher Education

John Tomasi sets the stage by diagnosing the state of play in recent thinking about viewpoint diversity. On one side are expertise-based defenders of the status quo; on the other are critics calling for proportional ideological representation. As an alternative to these two dominant takes on viewpoint diversity—cloistered orthodoxy and societal representation—Tomasi offers a framework for understanding how universities can foster genuine dialogue across differences without sacrificing academic standards. Subsequent essays delve into specific aspects: Nadine Strossen underscores the constitutional roots of viewpoint diversity in safeguarding liberty and democracy; Tyler VanderWeele discusses how to respond to the current problem of ideological homogeneity without undermining academic integrity; Jonathan Zimmerman emphasizes the importance of cultivating a culture of teaching that truly models and practices free inquiry. Others in this section explore the culture of campus debates, the role of faculty, and the vital need to resist censorship and dogmatism, especially in an era rife with political manipulation and social polarization.

Some skepticism toward the optimistic take on ubiquitous viewpoint diversity also surfaces in this section. Mark Bauerlein offers a cautionary perspective, warning that the very idea of "diversity" can sometimes be used to mask ideological conformity or superficial pluralism. Bret Stephens argues that some propositions threaten societal cohesion and moral decency, and that a commitment to diversity must be balanced with a responsibility to uphold certain moral and ethical boundaries. Together, Bauerlein and Stephens remind us that the pursuit of viewpoint diversity must be thoughtful, principled, and attentive to context. In the section's final essay, Hollis Robbins argues that the landscape of viewpoint diversity shifts dramatically with AI. While AI tools enable unprecedented access to diverse ideas, they also threaten authenticity by providing "pseudo-diversity"—responses that lack true conviction, nuance, and human responsibility.

Part II: Viewpoint Diversity in Society and Politics

Yascha Mounk illuminates the paradox of infinite sources of viewpoints available today—through social media and AI—while societal consensus and trust in institutions decline. He argues that the stratification of society along lines of education and income have created a disconnect: Expert classes and ordinary citizens inhabit vastly different worlds of belief and confidence and that to make these worldviews relatable becomes one of today's urgent imperatives. Ilana Redstone highlights the "viewpoint diversity paradox": that genuine democratic engagement must navigate the tension between allowing free expression and avoiding harmful content—an impossible task without understanding intent and reasoning. John Inazu emphasizes that a culture of confident pluralism is essential for sustaining both civil society and democratic institutions, underscoring that, beyond merely tolerating diversity, society must actively nurture a moral and practical ethic of respectful engagement to truly bridge divides and uphold democratic ideals. Danielle Allen emphasizes the importance of cultivating confident pluralists—individuals committed to listening, humility, and civility—in order to sustain a functioning democracy. She advocates five core virtues: reflection, institutional trust, compromise, listening, and dignity, which together foster resilient social bonds amid deep disagreements.

Part III: Viewpoint Diversity in Literature and Publishing

Bernard Schweizer critically examines how the ideal of literary diversity has been undermined by the very mechanisms supposed to promote it—namely, identity-based gatekeeping, sensitivity readers, and ideological curation, particularly by Amazon. These practices, he argues, lead to a flattening of literary expression and a suppression of authentic, complex narratives. Richard North Patterson offers a compelling case against the censorship of authors based on identity, highlighting how prejudice and ideological restrictions threaten the very freedom to imagine that literature embodies. Henry Louis Gates Jr. echoes this theme, emphasizing that the "freedom to write" is essential for marginalized voices to challenge history and shape society. Together, these essays reaffirm that literature must remain a space for authentic human storytelling, free from ideologically motivated bans and performative sensitivities.

Across all these essays, the common thread is an urgent need to reaffirm core values—belief in liberal democracy, the importance of moral humility, and the unbounded pursuit of truth—against a backdrop of rising censorship, ideological conformity, and technological disruption. Whether through fostering genuine debate on campuses, resisting the tendency to silo readers and writers by identity, or embracing the complex realities of a digital age, the volume advocates for a culture of bold, respectful, and open inquiry. It challenges readers—including educators, policymakers, authors, and citizens—to embody the virtues of confident pluralism: humility, perseverance, and the moral courage to engage deeply and humbly with the diversity of human experience. Only through such an ethic can society hope to sustain the democratic ideals of free speech, mutual understanding, and human dignity in a fractured and rapidly evolving world.

I

Viewpoint Diversity in Higher Education

The Heterodox View of Viewpoint Diversity

by John Tomasi

Every scholar endorses viewpoint diversity. Disagreement is the fuel on which the academic enterprise runs. If scholars all held the same view on every topic under study in the humanities, social sciences, and STEM fields, publication and scholarship would end. Even Lisa Siraganian, a self-styled critic of viewpoint diversity, concludes a broadside against that concept by acknowledging this fact: Scholarly thinking "benefits from exposure to different ideas."[1]

So, the question is not whether scholarship requires a diversity of viewpoints. The question is: *How much* viewpoint diversity do we need? Since most of the heat around this question concerns the appropriate range of ideological diversity, I shall focus on that issue. What degree of *ideological diversity* does responsible scholarship and teaching require?

Public records studies reveal that the professoriate has been steadily skewing ever more heavily left than right. Without any course-correction, that trend looks set to increase, perhaps

For discussion of these ideas, I am especially grateful to Micheal Regnier, Jonathan Haidt, Nicole Barbaro, Alex Arnold, Eric Torres, and Daniel Sargent. I presented drafts of this paper at Heterodox Academy's Segal Center for Academic Pluralism and at the Peregrine Collective at UC Berkeley.

dramatically. According to studies gathered by John Ellis, the ratio of left-leaning to right-leaning tenure-line professors was roughly 2:1 in 1969; 5:1 in 1999; 8:1 in 2015—and among junior professors, that ratio now stands at a whopping 49:1.[2] As Sam Abrams has documented, studies showing a wide imbalance between liberal and conservative professors have been replicated across many disciplines as well across the professoriate as a whole.[3] No serious scholar disputes the fact of a growing imbalance.

The increasing ideological homogeneity of the professoriate has been accompanied by a contraction in the range of ideas that students encounter in the classroom, as demonstrated by a recent national study of undergraduate syllabi.[4] Most alarming, the study finds, this narrowing range of viewpoints presented to students has occurred especially on hot-button issues on which mutual understanding and bridge-building presumably are most needed: the conflict between Israel and Palestine, racial bias in the criminal justice system, and abortion.

Although no serious scholar disputes the ideological imbalance of the professoriate, people do dispute the significance of this fact. There are at present two main views about viewpoint diversity—each locked in opposition to the other.

On one side are defenders of the *status quo*, such as Lisa Siraganian and the American Association of University Professors (AAUP). In the face of the facts just mentioned, they reject the idea that the academy today suffers from any "viewpoint diversity problem" at all. Defenders of (their own) expertise, this side says the range of viewpoint diversity within the academy should be whatever the cohort of professors currently inhabiting the university deems fit. Since the existing ideological distribution within the academy arose through processes of scholarly decision-making (the professoriate's own hiring and promotion decisions, the selection of research topics, the range of readings assigned in their classes, etc.), that distribution is therefore legitimate. The process of applied expertise *sanctifies* the product—whatever distribution might be produced.

On the other side are those who see the disparity between left- and right-leaning professors as a problem, while viewing that problem in explicitly political terms. This side sees the imbalance within the academy as a kind of injustice, the effective capture of a set of publicly funded institutions by one political party for its own benefit. Since the university system is entrusted with producing research that informs political decision-making, as well [as?] being tasked with educating the next generation of citizens, any ideological imbalance within the academy is a matter of public concern. As a remedy, they seek a political imposition of more balance within the political orientation of the professoriate, so that the ratio more closely (or at least less distantly) represents the political beliefs of the surrounding society.

These two views dominate debates about viewpoint diversity today. I am skeptical of both. But I also believe that we have something to learn from each. Seeing what is right (and wrong) about these two views points the way towards a third view. This view would bring intellectual humility to the claims of expertise, while reconciling the claims of ordinary politics to the special nature of the university.

1. The Scholarly Sanctification View

How wide a range of viewpoints should be welcomed on our university campuses? In the flagship publication of AAUP (American Association of University Professors), *Academe*, Lisa Siraganian offers a provocative answer to this question: The university should be exactly as viewpoint diverse as the professors who currently inhabit it think fit, and no more.[5] She explicitly criticizes Heterodox Academy, and me, for advocating a wider range of viewpoints. I'll return to that point. For now, notice that while I just described Siraganian's thesis as provocative, until very recently there was nothing at all provocative about her view.

Indeed, for decades Siraganian's thesis served as a rarely questioned academic state of affairs.

The concept of viewpoint diversity burst on the political scene in 2002 with the publication of David Horowitz's "Academic Bill of Rights." Noting the increasingly one-sided political party orientation of the professoriate, Horowitz argued that universities should seek greater pluralism and diversity. Although Horowitz used the phrase "intellectual pluralism," it was the term "viewpoint diversity" that captured the popular imagination (an n-gram of that phrase from 2002–2004, measuring popular usage, resembles the steep face of Mont Blanc).

By 2003, the AAUP's Committee A had issued a response to Horowitz. Their conclusion was that "decisions concerning the quality of scholarship and teaching are to be made by reference to the standards of the academic profession, as interpreted and applied by the community of scholars who are qualified by expertise and training to establish such standards."[6] How wide a range of views and opinions should be studied and taught on our campuses? Siraganian in 2025 and Committee A in 2003 agree: Universities should study and teach a range of viewpoints that is as wide, and no wider, than whatever group of professors currently inhabit the university believes appropriate.

As I'll explain in a moment, I find this approach implausible. But I share two key premises with Siraganian and the AAUP. The first is that the primary purpose of the university is the pursuit, preservation, and dissemination of knowledge. The second is that disciplinary standards are central to that purpose. Expertise matters, and any serious view of viewpoint diversity should recognize that. So far, so good.

The problem, however, is that there is a hidden third premise that Siraganian and the AAUP also rely upon to defend the *status quo*. This is the assumption that when people pass through the process of training and professionalization needed to enter the professoriate, they somehow leave behind the psychological biases and vulnerabilities to groupthink that are part of human nature. Siraganian and the AAUP believe that the process of academic professionalization sanctifies the collective decision-making of the professoriate. Thus, whatever decisions the professoriate makes about hiring and promotion, and whatever overall pattern emerges from those decisions, are *ipso facto* justified by the fact that the pattern arose through professors exercising their professional expertise.

As the AAUP statement put it in 2003: "The appropriate diversity of a university faculty must ultimately be conceived as a question of academic judgement". So, if an overall pattern emerges across the academy in which conservative and libertarian scholarship and reading assignments become ever more marginalized, as has happened, this is nothing to worry about—so long as each decision leading to that pattern was made according the existing professors' own expert judgment. There is no *external* standard that could be used to explain why the ideological narrowing of the academy might be anything to worry about. The opinion of the professors currently in the academy controls all: It alone defines the acceptable limits of viewpoint diversity.

As Jonathan Haidt and I have argued, this view is naïve, unhistorical, and strangely uncritical.[7] Professional training does not make professors immune to ordinary human biases.[8] Academics remain human still. And if the ideological boundaries and assumptions of the profession happen to align with the *professors' own* ideological boundaries—as can happen when the range of viewpoints in a group shrinks—they may be especially susceptible to bias. Today's cohort of scholarly experts remains vulnerable to the same "tyranny of public opinion" and "uncritical and intemperate partisanship" that the founders of the American Academy of University Professors in 1915 warned academia to resist.[9]

This idea, that professionalization does not insulate one from bias, is a major finding from the sociology of science. Indeed, recognition of the danger of bias can be seen in core academic practices, such as the doctrine of blind review, or the practice of selecting tenure letter writers from a diverse pool. These practices implicitly recognize that even academic experts remain subject to bias. The cohort of professors who currently inhabit the university remain *human*, just like every cohort before them and every cohort yet to come.

2. The Political Representation View

Since the filter of scholarly expertise will always remain flawed by human bias, one alternative would be to discard that filter altogether. Siraganian characterizes one such alternative as follows: "The more views you have, the more viewpoint diversity you have."[10] Whether the view is that the structure of DNA is a triple helix, or the claim that Maoist collective farming was an economic success, or the thesis that the earth is flat and the moon is square, this approach to viewpoint diversity says *the more views the better*.

The problem with this view is that if you only care about having the greatest number and variety of views, even when expert opinion has decisively shown those views to be false, one loses the connection to truth-seeking, which is the university's purpose. Yet there is a second problem with this view: To my knowledge, no one holds it.

Because she considers and rejects an implausible alternative to the AAUP's "simple-sanctification" view, Siraganian fails to consider a more serious alternative that stands closely *adjacent to* the straw man she sets up. This view, like the-more-views-the-better view that Siraganian considers, also rejects that AAUP claim to absolute sovereignty of whatever cohort of humans currently inhabit that professoriate. But it then looks to an external standard to determine when or if the decisions by the professoriate have gone astray.

This view, widely associated with the political right, says that the range of views under active discussion within the academy should be (broadly) representative of the political views held in the wider society—say, as represented by the major political parties. I'll call this view of viewpoint diversity the *political representation* view.

On the political representation view, if a society is divided roughly equally between people holding conservative and progressive political ideologies, that same range of views ought to be represented in the academy.

Like the principle that "the-more-views-the-better," the representation view uses an "expertise-free" criterion to decide how diverse the views in the university ought to be. Only by this approach, the boundaries of viewpoint diversity within the academy are tied to political representation.

Anyone who, like me, sees the university as fundamentally committed to knowledge-seeking, must reject this view—at least in this simple version. For one thing, if we believe the telos of the university is the search for knowledge, we should expect (indeed, *hope for*) the occasional achievement of scholarly consensus—even, perhaps, on contested political and moral issues. Further, why would we think having a faculty with more registered Republicans, say, would improve research and teaching in engineering, mathematics, or any other fields? And even within disciplines that do address political topics, why think that representation of the dominant political parties (in any one country, at any one historical moment) should be allowed to set the parameters of scholarly investigation? If our guide is knowledge-seeking, this simple version of the representative view is unattractive.

3. A Third Way: The Heterodox View

The purely internal, expertise-based view of viewpoint diversity—the scholarly sanctification view—is psychologically naïve. And the purely external view—the political representation view—likewise would weaken the commitment of universities to their knowledge-seeking function, just in a different way. So, what is to be done?

At Heterodox Academy, we believe there is a world out there worth knowing, and that disciplinary methods and standards—whatever their defects in practice—are our best chance of gaining that knowledge. Yet we also believe that the rising ideological conformity of the professoriate poses a threat to effective knowledge-seeking, and to the public credibility of our universities as well. This is a threat that the self-governing professoriate, so far, has shown itself unable (or unwilling) to address. But is there a way to capture both these insights in a single account of viewpoint diversity?

I believe there is, and here is the core idea: On every scholarly topic, the tools, norms, and standards of the relevant discipline generate a range of positions that might possibly be considered and defended by experts in that field (each according to their discipline's evidentiary standards). What is wanted is that a robust range of options on this methodologically identified "frontier" of positions be kept open *in a lively way*.

To achieve the good of viewpoint diversity in the sense I am proposing, it's not necessary that every thesis on that range of possibilities is actively being defended within the academy. Many questions—the shape of the earth, the outcome of Mao's agricultural reforms—have been decisively settled. We may have reason to teach *about* those questions, but the questions themselves have been settled. Expertise must be given its due.

Yet, from the other side, it is also not necessary that the defense of that (methodologically available) range of theses be politically representative of society. Universities are not essentially political institutions: They are essentially knowledge-seeking ones. Yet intellectual humility teaches us that the opinions of people outside the university can sometimes help us identify systemic biases and blind spots of scholars working within. Even experts sometimes need someone to tell them to check their premises.

This third view of viewpoint diversity is a kind of hybrid of the two dominant views—the scholarly sanctification view, and the political representation view. With its respect for disciplinary standards of evidence, it cares very much for "*doxa*," or truth-seeking beliefs. Yet, with its sharp awareness of the vulnerability to groupthink, even of knowledge-seekers, it also has a special concern for difference, or "*heteros*." I hope it will not surprise you that I call this third view the *heterodox view* of viewpoint diversity.

On the heterodox approach to viewpoint diversity, as I have said, what we need is that the methodologically available range of research questions be kept open in a lively way. And this, precisely, is where many of us fear the contemporary university has fallen short.

Consider a few examples. Climate science has a set of methodologies (ways of presenting evidence) that allow for the generation of a range of climate change models. Some predictive models are "hotter" and "faster"; some models are "cooler" and "slower." To have healthy viewpoint diversity in climate science, we don't need to have each possible predictive position being defended. Nor do we need to have an "ideological balance" across the range. Again, some degree of scientific convergence is a reasonable academic goal. But if climate science falls into a position where certain (methodologically available) positions cannot even be discussed, then we have failed on the viewpoint diversity standard.

Similarly, the field of international affairs has a set of methodologies that make available a range of positions about the proper relation of (let's say) the United States of America to the rest of the world. If a scholarly consensus emerges around a liberal internationalist (or cosmopolitan) answer to that question, that's fine. Again, we are searching for knowledge. But if rival methodologically possible positions (say, the doctrine of American exceptionalism) cannot even be discussed or taught in a serious way, then we have fallen short on viewpoint diversity in our sense.

So too with political or intellectual history. Having lots of scholars writing books that explore the wisdom of Franklin Roosevelt or John F. Kennedy or Ruth Bader Ginsburg is fine. But if scholars committed to those same historical standards of evidence cannot even consider writing a similarly positive book about, say, Calvin Coolidge or Ronald Reagan or Clarence Thomas, then something has gone seriously wrong. The scope of viewpoint diversity has been artificially narrowed, and our ability to search for knowledge has been weakened as a result.

Similarly with medicine and public health. If, during a pandemic, a public health consensus emerges and stabilizes on masking, lockdowns, and vaccines, so be it. But if heterodox positions about pandemic responses—such as the Great Barrington Declaration—cannot even be stated without attacks on the character or motives of dissenting scholars, such that arguments for those alternatives cannot even be considered according to disciplinary standards of evidence, then something has gone wrong with the discipline of public health from a viewpoint diversity perspective.

This heterodox model of viewpoint diversity could also encapsulate yet another form of viewpoint diversity that some defend: identity viewpoint diversity. Many people demand more racial or gender diversity on campus as a requirement of (their theory of) social justice. There are important moral issues here. Now, the heterodox ideal of viewpoint diversity, by contrast, would advocate greater identity diversity precisely because (and precisely when) greater racial or gender diversity opens up hidden (methodologically available) views and research programs, thus making neglected options available in a lively way.

For example, the late twentieth century saw a flowering of historical scholarship on the American Founding Period (Gordon Wood's 1969 epic *The Creation of the American Republic*,

1776–1787 is an exemplar). But while historians of this era produced brilliant and illuminating works about the principles and achievements of the leading agents of America's founding era, the historical role and experience of enslaved Black people in early America, and of other marginalized groups, was hardly mentioned at all. As university faculties and student bodies became more racially integrated in the 1980s and 1990s, historians of early America increasingly turned their attention to those neglected perspectives and experiences—thus potentially enriching historical scholarship and teaching alike. Identity diversity, in this case, had the potential to increase the breadth and power of viewpoint diversity in our sense.

So, we have considered and rejected two "pure" approaches to viewpoint diversity. One, the scholarly sanctification view, is purely *internal*. It asserts that the boundaries of viewpoint diversity on campus should be set entirely by whatever cohort of academics presently inhabit the academy—no matter their susceptibility to groupthink and cognitive bias. The other, the political representation view, is purely *external*. It asserts that the boundaries of viewpoints on campus should be set in a way this is politically representative of the wider society—no matter that some of those views and opinions (from both sides) are demonstrably false.

As we have seen, neither of these "pure" approaches can plausibly answer the question with which we started: In a university committed primarily to the search for knowledge, how diverse should viewpoint diversity be? In response, I am proposing a hybrid view of viewpoint diversity, one that seeks to pick up an insight from each of those views while avoiding their defects. On this, the heterodox view of viewpoint diversity, what is wanted is that a robust range of (methodologically available) ideas and opinions be kept open in a lively way.

Siraganian writes: "[T]hose of us who want good ideas to win and bad ideas to lose should understand that viewpoint diversity will not get us there."[11] The opposite is true. If we are to have any hope that good ideas will win and bad ideas will lose, we need a wider range of views to be kept open in a lively way at our universities. As the examples mentioned above demonstrate, such views often arise from real debates occurring in the surrounding society—not just from intramural scholarly discourse. Views kept open in this way do not get a free pass simply *because* they are different from mainstream views of the professoriate at any given moment. Nor do they have any special standing for that reason. But nor do such views get shut down without examination. Instead, for views to be kept open in a lively way means that such views are welcomed into the field of disciplinary contestation, where they will be judged, and must be defended, according to disciplinary methodologies and standards of evidence.

This is a heterodox, knowledge-tracking approach to viewpoint diversity. It recognizes that group opinions, even of experts, can sometimes go badly wrong. While firmly committed to disciplinary methods and standards of evidence, this heterodox approach also reflects a form of intellectual humility appropriate to scholars, who should be ready to recognize that, despite all their degrees and qualifications, they sometimes have things to learn from people who live and work and form opinions outside the ivory tower.

Notes

1 Lisa Siraganian, "Viewpoint Diversity Is a MAGA Plot," The Chronicle of Higher Education, October 10, 2025, https://www.chronicle.com/article/viewpoint-diversity-is-a-maga-plot.

2 *The Breakdown of Higher Education: How It Happened, the Damage It Does, and What Can Be Done* (New York: Encounter Books, 2021), 25–36 and 163.

3 Samuel J. Abrams, "Seven Theses for Viewpoint Diversity," *Minding the Campus*, Oct 2, 2025, https://www.mindingthecampus.org/2025/10/02/seven-theses-for-viewpoint-diversity/.

4 Emma Pettit, "These Scholarly Topics Are Hotley Debated. So Why Don't Syllabi Reflect That?" Chronicle of Higher Education, July 22,

2025, https://www.chronicle.com/article/these-scholarly-topics-are-hotly-debated-so-why-dont-syllabi-reflect-that; Jon A. Shields, Yuval Avnur, and Stephanie Muravchick, "Closed Classrooms? An Analysis of College Syllabi on Contentious Issues," Working Paper (July 10, 2025); https://www.persuasion.community/p/we-analyzed-university-syllabi-theres.

5 Lisa Siraganian, "Seven Theses Against Viewpoint Diversity: The problems with arguments for intellectual pluralism," *Academe*, Fall 2025, https://www.aaup.org/academe/issues/fall-2025/seven-theses-against-viewpoint-diversity.

6 Academic Bill of Rights, AAUP, https://www.aaup.org/reports-publications/aaup-policies-reports/topical-reports/academic-bill-rights.

7 John Tomasi and Jonathan Haidt, "Universities Can't Pursue Truth Without Viewpoint Diversity," *Inside Higher Education*, October 29, 2025, https://www.insidehighered.com/opinion/views/2025/10/29/you-cant-pursue-truth-without-viewpoint-diversity-opinion.

8 On taboos: https://journals.sagepub.com/doi/full/10.1177/17456916241252085; on blind spots: https://journals.sagepub.com/doi/10.1177/09637214231178745; on groupthink: https://www.nature.com/articles/s41562–025-02153–1; on the politicization of scientific standards: https://www.cambridge.org/core/journals/behavioral-and-brain-sciences/article/abs/political-diversity-will-improve-social-psychological-science1/A54AD4878AED1AFC8BA6AF54A890149F.

9 "1915 Declaration of Principles on Academic Freedom and Academic Tenure," American Association of University Professors: https://www.aaup.org/NR/rdonlyres/A6520A9D-0A9A-47B3-B550-C006B5B224E7/0/1915Declaration.pdf.

10 Siraganian, "Seven Theses Against Viewpoint Diversity."

11 Siraganian, "Seven Theses Against Viewpoint Diversity."

Viewpoint Diversity as a Core Constitutional Value, Central to Liberty, Equality, and Democracy

by Nadine Strossen

Viewpoint diversity is literally the "bedrock"[1]—the Supreme Court's term—of our cherished First Amendment freedom of speech. In an often-cited 1949 decision, the Court declared: "The right to speak freely and to promote diversity of ideas and programs is . . . one of the chief distinctions that sets us apart from totalitarian regimes."[2] Viewpoint diversity is also foundational for rights that are closely associated with freedom of speech: the freedoms of thought, conscience, belief, and association; and academic freedom. For example, in a pathbreaking 1967 academic freedom case, the Court proclaimed: "The Nation's future depends upon leaders trained through wide exposure to that robust exchange of ideas which discovers truth 'out of a multitude of tongues, rather than through any kind of authoritative selection.'"[3] This statement recognizes that viewpoint diversity is as essential for democracy as it is for liberty. And viewpoint diversity is also integral to equality, as the Court has recognized in many decisions that bar government discrimination against speakers based on either their identities or their ideas.

The Supreme Court long has stressed that these interrelated core constitutional values—"liberty and justice for all"—are especially important in our nation's educational institutions, for individuals and our society alike, because these institutions "are educating the young for citizenship," and thus require "scrupulous protection of Constitutional freedoms . . . if we are not to strangle the free mind at its source and teach youth to discount important principles of our government as mere platitudes."[4]

Indeed, the Court has used apocalyptic language to describe the adverse national consequences that would result from reduced viewpoint diversity in our educational institutions. For example, in an important 1957 decision, the Court warned: "To impose any strait jacket upon the intellectual leaders in our colleges and universities would imperil the future of our Nation. . . . Teachers and students must always remain free to inquire . . . to gain new understanding; otherwise, our civilization will stagnate and die."[5]

Given the special significance of viewpoint diversity for our nation's campuses and schools, it is not surprising that most challenges to it have arisen in the educational context, which is therefore the focus of this essay. These challenges have come from both ends of the ideological spectrum.

On the Left, ongoing challenges to viewpoint diversity trace back to the rise of critical race theory (CRT) and other identity-based academic frameworks in the latter decades of the twentieth century. Proponents of these approaches have argued that robust free speech rights, which extend even to hateful or discriminatory views, endanger equality rights for members of racial, ethnic, and other Identitarian minority groups. This perspective continues to hold sway on the many campuses that enforce hate speech codes in various guises, including through overly broad definitions of "hostile environment harassment" (sometimes labeled "discriminatory harassment").

To be sure, government may restrict hateful or harassing speech when the restriction is not based solely on disapproval of the speech's viewpoint, but rather is based on other, contextual factors: if the speech directly causes certain specific serious harm, such as intentionally threatening or bullying a specifically targeted individual; or If the speech violates a reasonable, viewpoint-neutral time, place, or manner regulation. In particular, the Supreme Court has said that expression may be restricted as hostile environment harassment if—but only if—it satisfies multiple contextual factors: It must be "so severe, pervasive, and objectively offensive that it effectively bars the victim's access to an educational opportunity or benefit."[6]

In contrast with contextually circumscribed concepts of impermissible hateful or harassing speech, the distorted concept that has been prevalent on campus is viewpoint-based and has been wielded to suppress views that diverge from campus orthodoxy on many important topics, including abortion, DEI (diversity, equity, and inclusion), gender/sexuality, and Israel–Palestine.

Officials in the Obama, Biden, and Trump administrations alike have pressured federally funded educational institutions (a category that includes virtually all educational institutions, both public and private) to enforce exaggerated concepts of punishable harassing expression against certain views that each administration has disfavored. Both the Obama and Biden administrations invoked Title IX of the Education Amendments of 1972 to suppress disfavored views about sex and gender. And in response to post–October 7 pro-Palestinian campus protests, both the Biden and Trump administrations have invoked Title VI of the 1964 Civil Rights Act to suppress disfavored views about Israel–Palestine.

Beyond the misuse of Title VI to suppress antisemitic and anti-Israeli viewpoints, Donald Trump and others from the right end of the political spectrum have wielded many other government powers to restrict and chill these viewpoints, as well as other viewpoints they disfavor.[7] For example, while Trump and other right-of-center critics of "woke" campus ideology (such as pro-CRT or pro-DEI ideas) have assailed the suppression of non-woke viewpoints, these critics have pursued many measures that share the same fundamental flaw—the stifling of viewpoint diversity—simply substituting one set of preferred orthodoxies (such as anti-CRT or anti-DEI ideas) for another.

It is especially ironic that various Trump-advocated measures that purport to require campuses to promote viewpoint diversity in fact have the opposite impact. A prime example is the Trump administration's broad, vague commands to Harvard University that "each department, field, or teaching unit must be individually viewpoint diverse"[8]—in effect, a license for the federal officials enforcing this decree to suppress whatever viewpoints they dislike, while promoting their own preferred views. As Northwestern University Law Professor John McGinnis, a prominent conservative, wrote: "[S]uch a requirement would replace the spontaneous, merit-based competition of ideas with coercive bureaucratic allocation and grant the government dangerous power over thought."[9]

Despite the pronounced ideological differences among the three most recent presidents, they all have enforced policies that reflect the key anti–viewpoint diversity argument that was initially advanced by left-wing CRT proponents: that equality for certain (identitarian) campus minority groups is undermined by free speech in general, and by its core viewpoint diversity requirement in particular, since that requirement entails protection of discriminatory expression. Specifically, the Obama and Biden administrations embraced this argument by suppressing (allegedly) misogynistic or transphobic expression as illegal discrimination against women or trans people. And the Biden and Trump administrations have embraced that argument by suppressing (allegedly) antisemitic and anti-Israeli government expression as illegal discrimination against Jews or Israelis.

An accurate understanding of viewpoint diversity demonstrates that it is essential not only for free speech, but also equality. Experience confirms that unless we protect equality for all ideas—the equal right of all ideas to be aired and considered—we cannot promote equality for all people. Correspondingly, permitting government to selectively restrict disfavored views simultaneously empowers government to selectively restrict disfavored speakers. Therefore, to promote campuses that are truly diverse, equal, and inclusive with respect to all people, we must ensure that campuses are truly diverse, equal, and inclusive with respect to all viewpoints[10]—and vice versa.

This essay develops the themes outlined above. Part I explains the key role of viewpoint diversity in First Amendment law. Part II highlights the Supreme Court's special solicitude for viewpoint diversity in the educational context. Part III elaborates on why viewpoint diversity is as essential for democracy and equality as it is for individual liberty.

1. The Key Role of Viewpoint Diversity in First Amendment Law

Although the precise phrase "viewpoint diversity" is not a constitutional law term of art, the concept it captures is deeply embedded in First Amendment law, tracing back to the Supreme Court's earliest landmark free speech rulings in the 1940s.[11] One notable example is the 1949 *Terminiello* decision quoted above, in which the Court celebrated the "diversity of ideas" that free speech "promote[s]."[12] In a much-quoted 1989 decision, the Court hailed this concept as the "bedrock"[13] principle underlying our cherished free speech rights.

Starting in the 1970s, the Court began to use the phrases "viewpoint neutrality" or "content neutrality" as constitutional law terms of art, to summarize the government's (including any public educational institution's[14]) paramount duty concerning expression by members of the public:[15] Government must remain neutral regarding the expression's viewpoint—its content, messages, and ideas—neither favoring nor disfavoring speech based on official or public support for or opposition to any viewpoint.

The Supreme Court has issued many eloquent encomiums to the foundational viewpoint neutrality principle. One important example comes from the Court's unanimous 1972 *Chicago v. Mosley* decision. Given the overlapping anti-discrimination values that link the constitutional rights of free speech and equality, it is noteworthy that this landmark free speech opinion was authored by Justice Thurgood Marshall, the Court's first Black justice, who had headed the NAACP (National Association for the Advancement of Colored People) Legal Defense and Educational Fund. Flagging the equal freedom that our Constitution ensures for "each individual" and for "any thought," Justice Marshall declared:

> Above all else, the First Amendment means that government has no power to restrict expression because of its message, its ideas, its subject matter, or its content. To permit the continued building of our politics and culture, and to assure self-fulfillment for each individual, our people are guaranteed the right to express any thought, free from government censorship.[16]

No matter how deeply and widely loathed "any thought" might be, this does not justify censoring it. Rather, we must use alternative means to counter the message, including education and persuasion.

As Justice Marshall indicated in *Mosley*, the rationale for the viewpoint neutrality rule is precisely to promote viewpoint diversity among "We the People"—to prevent government from prescribing which views are acceptable, instead allowing individuals to make those determinations for themselves. In short, in order to promote viewpoint diversity among individual citizens, government must practice viewpoint neutrality. (The same rationale undergirds campus institutional neutrality policies regarding all issues not central to the university's own core mission, such as the University of Chicago's famous 1967 "Kalven principles": to promote viewpoint diversity among individual members of the campus community, university officials must remain neutral—*i.e.*, silent—about such issues.)

The longstanding First Amendment commitment to viewpoint neutrality on the government's part—and the resulting viewpoint diversity on the citizenry's part—was most memorably enshrined in the landmark 1943 case, *West Virginia Board of Education v. Barnette*.[17]

Barnette expressly affirmed "the ideal of . . . political neutrality" for "public education," requiring that it "will not be partisan or enemy of any class, creed, party, or faction."[18]

Barnette struck down state laws compelling public school students to salute the US flag and recite the Pledge of Allegiance. These laws had been challenged by members of the Jehovah's Witnesses religious denomination, who believed that the challenged exercises constituted idolatry, violating the biblical Second Commandment. Given the religious nature of the Witnesses' beliefs, the Court could have protected their rights specifically under the First Amendment's Free Exercise Clause, which shields "the free exercise of religion." Instead, though, the Court's rationale reflected universal concerns about freedom of belief, conscience, and thought more generally. In one of the most widely quoted statements the Court has ever issued, it proclaimed: "If there is any fixed star in our constitutional constellation, it is that no official, high or petty, can prescribe what shall be orthodox in politics, nationalism, religion, or other matters of opinion."[19]

The mandatory flag salute laws were enacted to promote a supremely important public purpose: national unity and security when the US was engaged in World War II. Thus, it is especially significant that the Court nevertheless held that even this purpose could not legitimate government infringements on freedom of conscience. Underscoring that the First Amendment "right to differ"—in other words, to express diverse viewpoints—extends even to supremely important matters, another justly famous *Barnette* passage stated: "[F]reedom to differ is not limited to things that do not matter much. That would be a mere shadow of freedom. The test of its substance is the right to differ as to things that touch the heart of the existing order."[20]

Barnette stands as an especially instructive monument to viewpoint diversity because of its extensive discussion of the opposite of such diversity, which the government invoked as assertedly justifying the mandatory flag salute and pledge. Not surprisingly, the government described this countervailing concern not as promoting "orthodoxy," with its negative connotations, but rather as promoting "national unity," which had positive connotations, especially when the US was engaged in a world war against fascist, genocidal regimes. While recognizing the value of national unity, the Court powerfully explained why such unity is ultimately undermined by speech regulations that coerce uniformity of expression. To the contrary, the Court described how the unity that our Constitution embodies depends on individual freedom to express—or not express—diverse views:

> National unity, as an end which officials may foster by persuasion and example, is not in question. The problem is whether, under our Constitution, compulsion . . . is a permissible means for its achievement. . . . As governmental pressure toward unity becomes greater, so strife becomes more bitter. . . . Ultimate futility of such attempts . . . is the lesson of every such effort from the Roman drive to stamp out Christianity . . . down to the fast failing efforts of our present totalitarian enemies.[21]

As this passage notes, far from effectively promoting national unity, restrictions on viewpoint diversity, to the contrary, foment "strife." Moreover, the opinion observed that especially corrosive divisions are caused by the very type of anti-viewpoint-diversity regulations that this essay is discussing: regulations in the educational context. As the Court wrote: "Probably no deeper division of our people could proceed from any provocation than from . . . choos[ing] what doctrine . . . public educational officials shall compel youth to unite in embracing."[22]

Beyond citing examples of past failed efforts to promote national unity by restricting viewpoint diversity, *Barnette* also professed faith that US unity and strength would be promoted instead by protecting "intellectual individualism" and "rich cultural diversities":

> [W]e [have] no fear that freedom to be intellectually and spiritually diverse or even contrary will disintegrate the social organization. To believe that patriotism will not flourish if patriotic ceremonies are voluntary and spontaneous, instead of a compulsory routine, is to make an unflattering estimate of the appeal of our institutions to free minds. We can have intellectual individualism and the rich cultural diversities that we owe to exceptional minds only at the price of occasional eccentricity and abnormal attitudes.[23]

Barnette's bar against government regulations that undermine viewpoint diversity has been enforced in many, varying situations, including in the educational context. For example, *Barnette* recently has been cited as proscribing the compelled statements that have been proliferating at universities and schools, at the behest of progressives: mandatory DEI statements on the part of applicants for faculty jobs or promotions, which describe the applicants' work to promote diversity, equity and inclusion;[24] and mandatory "land acknowledgment" statements on course syllabi, conveying the institution's official views about Native American property rights in the land it now occupies.

The nonpartisan, ideologically diverse Academic Freedom Alliance (AFA) has urged higher education institutions not to demand any such compulsory statements. Stating that "[t]he growing regime of . . . forced pledges of conformity threatens to impose a suffocating orthodoxy," the AFA stressed that these pledges "penaliz[e] expressions . . . across a wide ideological range that includes not only right-leaning scholars but left-leaning scholars as well." While endorsing campus "efforts to ensure" that "all members of their communities" can enjoy "environments free of bigotry," the AFA opposed "monitoring beliefs by demanding pledges of allegiance to . . . policies that are often vague, frequently ambiguous, and invariably controversial."[25]

Government can of course undermine viewpoint diversity by compelling silence, as well as by compelling speech. The Trump administration's requirement that universities must purge DEI-related terminology and concepts from their programs or forfeit federal funding is simply the flip side of the requirement that candidates for faculty positions must provide DEI statements or forfeit such positions. Both approaches squarely violate the viewpoint neutrality principle, hence eroding viewpoint diversity.

2. The Special Importance of Viewpoint Diversity in Educational Institutions

Barnette is one of many Court decisions that have consistently stressed the special importance of freedom of speech—and the core viewpoint neutrality/diversity values it embodies—in all educational institutions, from elementary schools through universities. Several additional such decisions have already been quoted. I will now confine myself to one further example: the Court's 1969 ruling in *Tinker v. Des Moines School District*,[26] which upheld the free speech rights of middle and high school students to convey diverse—*i.e.*, unpopular—views, opposing the Vietnam War.

Tinker reaffirmed the centrality of the viewpoint neutrality/diversity commitment for *all* educational institutions. For example, quoting prior decisions involving K-12 schools and universities alike, the Court stated: "The vigilant protection of constitutional freedoms is nowhere more vital than in the community of American schools. . . . The classroom is peculiarly the marketplace of ideas."[27] *Tinker* contained many eloquent passages amplifying on this theme, for instance: "[S]tudents may not be regarded as closed-circuit recipients of only that which the State chooses to communicate. They may not be confined to the expression of those sentiments that are officially approved."[28]

Tinker powerfully explained the fatal First Amendment flaws of measures that suppress controversial views in our educational institutions on the rationale that they cause "discomfort" or "divisiveness," as recent initiatives from both ends of the political spectrum have sought to do. Many progressives have invoked these concerns to suppress non-progressive perspectives on issues regarding race and gender; many conservatives have invoked these very same concerns to suppress progressive perspectives on those topics. (See examples cited above.)

The *Tinker* decision acknowledges the discomfort and divisiveness that speech can indeed cause whenever it diverges or dissents from prevailing views; these problems occurred in *Tinker* itself. That case arose in 1965 in Des Moines, Iowa, a time and place in which the Vietnam War was still very popular, with many local community members fighting and dying in the war. Therefore, the anti-war views that Mary Beth Tinker and several other students conveyed by wearing black armbands were not only politically unpopular, and even viewed as unpatriotic or treasonous; additionally, these views were perceived as insulting, disrespectful, and traumatizing to the members of their school community whose close relatives were fighting in Vietnam, and had even been injured and died there.

Tinker's protection of free speech and viewpoint diversity, notwithstanding their negative personal and community impacts, underscores the significance of these values. The Court forcefully explained why the freedom to express diverse views—even when they are despised and disturbing—ultimately serves positive ends for all of us individuals and our nation as a whole:

> Any variation from the majority's opinion may inspire fear. Any word spoken . . . that deviates from the views of another person may start an argument or cause a disturbance. But our Constitution says we must take this risk. . . . It is this sort of hazardous freedom—this kind of openness—that is the basis of our national strength and of the independence and vigor of Americans who grow up and live in this relatively permissive, often disputatious, society.[29]

3. Viewpoint Neutrality/Diversity Are Also Essential for Promoting Democracy and Equality

The decisions cited in the preceding section, focusing on educational institutions, highlight the important role that viewpoint diversity in those institutions plays in our democracy. This key theme was also stressed in the seminal *Barnette* decision. It memorably explained that the absence of viewpoint neutrality/diversity—*i.e.*, official "orthodoxy"—is as antithetical to our democratic self-government as it is to individual liberty: "We set up government by consent of the governed, and the Bill of Rights denies those in power any legal opportunity to coerce that consent. Authority here is to be controlled by public opinion, not public opinion by authority."[30] As a more recent Supreme Court opinion observed, viewpoint-discriminatory regulations subvert the sovereignty of "We the People" by empowering officials to "suppress unpopular ideas or information or manipulate public debate through coercion rather than persuasion."[31]

Justice Thurgood Marshall's *Mosley* opinion, quoted above, recognized that viewpoint-based speech restrictions also violate equality norms, because official discrimination against certain ideas entails discrimination against certain speakers. *Barnette* flagged this key point too: "Those who begin coercive elimination of dissent soon find themselves exterminating dissenters."[32]

The Court additionally acknowledged these intertwined

forms of discrimination—against ideas and individuals—in its 1951 *Niemotko v. Maryland*[33] ruling. *Niemotko* unanimously struck down a city's refusal to grant a Jehovah's Witnesses group a permit to use a park for Bible talks, even though it had granted such permits to other religious and political groups. The Court observed that "the permit was denied because of the city's dislike for or disagreement with the Witnesses." In fact, the Court expressly based its ruling on the Constitution's Equal Protection Clause, as well as the First Amendment (the *Mosley* decision did likewise).

The non-partisan campus-focused free speech organization FIRE (the Foundation for Individual Rights and Expression) has persuasively summarized the mutually reinforcing relationship between free speech and equality, between diversity/inclusivity of ideas and diversity/inclusivity of identities. In explaining why compulsory DEI statements violate both free speech and equality principles, FIRE stated:

> This is not a zero-sum game. The ideals of free speech and diversity/inclusivity need not live in tension; in fact, the latter depends on the former. To paraphrase former congressman and civil rights leader John Lewis, without freedom of speech and the right to dissent, any movement for genuine diversity and inclusion is a bird without wings. The most marginalized voices are those most in need of free speech protections. When universities uphold expressive freedom, they allow a diversity of voices and perspectives to flourish and create space for dialogue across lines of identity and ideology.[34]

Conclusion

This essay has demonstrated that the reciprocally reinforcing constitutional values of liberty, equality, and democracy are all fostered by viewpoint diversity, focusing on the preeminently important context of educational institutions. In recent decades, people (including officials) on both ends of the political spectrum have opposed viewpoint diversity on particular topics, seeking to suppress views that counter their preferred orthodoxies on those topics—notably, gender/sexuality, race, and Israel-Palestine.

This essay has explained why our educational institutions must include expression that conveys the full range of diverse ideas—including discriminatory ideas—as a prerequisite for including the full range of diverse people, and vice versa. While opponents of viewpoint diversity from across the ideological spectrum have argued that it promotes or even constitutes identity-based discrimination, the opposite is true: Viewpoint diversity is antithetical to such discrimination.

A meaningful, robust concept of DEI must encompass viewpoint diversity—contrary to the current prevalent practices.[35] This important insight has been stressed by Harvard University professor Danielle Allen, who was a co-chair of Harvard's Task Force on Inclusion and Belonging, appointed by Harvard's then-president Drew Faust in 2016. When the task force issued its report in 2018, Allen lauded its "breakthrough in thinking about these issues: the recognition that academic freedom and inclusion and belonging are mutually reinforcing values to be advanced simultaneously."[36]

In December 2023, in the wake of the much-criticized Congressional testimony by Harvard's president (as well as two other university presidents), and the widespread public concern about campus discrimination against certain people and certain expression, Allen wrote an op-ed entitled, "We've lost our way on campus. Here's how we can find our way back."[37] Lamenting that the task force report's "focus on academic freedom" had gone "largely overlooked by university administrators," Allen urged a renewed commitment to viewpoint diversity as "our way back" to truly inclusive campus communities: "I hope this moment gives all of us . . . a chance to course-correct. . . . The good news is we know how. A framework of confident pluralism—inclusion and belonging, academic freedom and mutual respect—offers a path forward."

I echo Allen's wise words, with one respectful amendment: "confident pluralism" offers *the* "path forward."

Notes

1 *Texas v. Johnson*, 491 U.S. 397, 414 (1989).

2 *Terminiello v. Chicago*, 337 U.S. 1, 4 (1949).

3 *Keyishian v. Board of Regents*, 385 U.S. 589, 603 (1967).

4 *West Virginia Board of Education v. Barnette*, 319 U.S. 624, 637 (1943).

5 *Sweezy v. New Hampshire*, 354 U.S. 234, 250 (1957).

6 *Davis v. Monroe County School District*, 526 U.S. 629 (1999).

7 *See, e.g.*, https://www.nytimes.com/2025/08/06/us/politics/stanford-lawsuit-student-activist-deportations.html (describing lawsuit brought in August 2025 by FIRE (the Foundation for Individual Rights and Expression), seeking to invalidate federal statute that the Trump administration has invoked to deport noncitizens for engaging in constitutionally protected speech, which has chilled expression by noncitizens, including faculty members and students.

8 "Read the Trump Administration's April 11 Demands to Harvard," *The Harvard Crimson*, April 15, 2025, https://www.thecrimson.com/article/2025/4/15/agencies-demands-to-harvard/.

9 "Columbia University Can Lead a New Era of Civil Rights," *Wall Street Journal*, August 1, 2025.

10 As explained above, the First Amendment does permit speech restrictions that are not based solely on disapproval of the speech's viewpoint.

11 Indeed, as far back as 1923, even before the Court had held states to be bound by the First Amendment's free speech guarantees, it relied on another constitutional provision to strike down a state law that barred the teaching of modern languages, stressing our national commitment to viewpoint diversity, and contrasting the US with Plato's ideal republic and ancient Sparta in this regard. *Meyer v. Nebraska*, 262 U.S. 390, 401–02 (the state's "desire . . . to foster a homogeneous people with American ideals . . . conflict[s] with [individual] rights"). Notably, the Court relied on the Fourteenth Amendment's general language, barring states from "depriv[ing] any person of . . . liberty without due process of law," deeming the right to a viewpoint-diverse education to be a "fundamental right,"

and "one of those privileges long recognized at common law as essential to the orderly pursuit of happiness by free men." *Id.* at 401, 399.

12 337 U.S. at 4.

13 *Texas v. Johnson*, 491 U.S. at 414.

14 Although the First Amendment doesn't directly constrain private educational institutions, almost all of them have voluntarily adopted policies that are consistent with First Amendment norms, to further their scholarly and teaching missions.

15 In contrast, when the government itself is the speaker—including when it deputizes others to speak on its behalf—it has no viewpoint neutrality obligation; to the contrary, it may espouse whatever views its officials favor. For members of the public who support differing views, the remedies are to try to persuade the officials or to vote them out of office.

16 *Police Department of Chicago v. Mosley*, 408 U.S. 92, 95 (1972).

17 319 U.S. 624 (1943).

18 *Id.* at 637.

19 *Id.* at 642.

20 *Id.*

21 *Id.* at 640–41.

22 *Id.* at 641.

23 *Id.* at 641–42.

24 Notwithstanding the Trump administration's pressures on campus to extirpate references to DEI, a comprehensive study that Heterodox Academy issued in August 2025 showed that 22.3 percent of 10,000+ faculty job listings in the 2024–25 US higher education hiring cycle requested DEI statements or other DEI-related material. See https://heterodoxacademy.org/reports/whats-going-on-with-dei-statements-in-faculty-hiring-analysis-of-faculty-job-ads-from-fall-2024/?utm_source=substack&utm_medium=email.

25 https://academicfreedom.org/wp-content/uploads/2022/08/AFA-DEI-Statement-081822.pdf.

26 393 US. 503 (1969).

27 *Id.* at 512, quoting *Keyishian*, 385 U.S. at 603 (1970); and *Shelton v. Tucker*, 364 U.S. 479, 487 (1960).

28 *Id.* at 508–09.

29 *Id.*

30 319 U.S. at 641.

31 *Turner Broadcasting System, Inc. v.* FCC, 512 U.S. 622, 641 (1994).

32 319 U.S. at 641.

33 340 U.S. 268 (1951).

34 https://www.thefire.org/research-learn/fire-statement-use-diversity-equity-and-inclusion-criteria-faculty-hiring-and.

35 *See* the August 2025 Heterodox Academy report cited in n. 24 above; it showed that only 15.6 percent of (the many) faculty job ads seeking diversity statements mention viewpoint diversity, suggesting that most campus efforts to improve diversity focus on diversity of identity, rather than ideas.

36 Marina N. Bolotnikiva, "$10 Million for a More Inclusive Faculty," *Harvard Magazine*, March 27, 2018, https://www.harvardmagazine.com/2018/03/diversity-task-force-report.

37 *The Washington Post*, December 10, 2023.

Higher Education Has a Viewpoint Diversity Problem—Here's How to Respond

by Tyler J. VanderWeele

(originally published in *The Harvard Crimson*, February 12, 2024)

In 2002, writer David Horowitz proposed an Academic Bill of Rights to ensure viewpoint diversity in US higher education. The proposal was criticized for not respecting the autonomy and scholarly standards of academic disciplines, and for attempting to force change from the top down.

The critics had a point, but I think his diagnosis of the problem was correct: Higher education struggles with respect for appropriate forms of viewpoint diversity.

For example, the imbalance in faculty political commitments has only grown in the intervening decades: By one measure, the liberal-to-conservative ratio of faculty in American universities increased from 2:1 in 1989 to 5:1 in 2017. According to a 2023 survey by *The Crimson*, among Harvard faculty, it now appears to stand at roughly 26:1.

If this lack of viewpoint diversity were simply due to the steady conquest of ignorance by knowledge, this would be worth celebrating. The reality, however, is that ideological or political homogeneity often just inhibits the pursuit of truth, sometimes causing entire areas of inquiry to be neglected. This hinders universities' missions of generating, preserving, and transmitting knowledge and preparing students for democratic citizenship.

As John Stuart Mill argued in "On Liberty," ignoring alternative viewpoints compromises our capacity to pursue truth, to understand other perspectives, to realize when we are wrong, and even to adequately defend our positions when right. Lack of intellectual diversity among faculty (and administrators) might also render open student discourse increasingly difficult, as indeed we experience at Harvard.

How do we explain the lack of intellectual diversity among faculty?

A central explanation may concern the research areas in which departments choose to hire. For example, in my own discipline of public health, I believe there would be opposition to faculty searches for experts on the relations between religion and health or marriage and health despite empirical evidence indicating their importance.

For many, the topics seem too closely associated with traditional values. I imagine similar dynamics are at play in many disciplines. As the ideological perspectives become more homogeneous, the topics considered important narrow, further reinforcing lack of intellectual diversity. It's a vicious cycle.

I don't believe universities should implement new quotas targeting ideological diversity, but I do think they should self-consciously diversify the research areas they target in faculty searches. I would put forward the following principle as one consideration, among many, that departments should weigh in faculty hiring:

When a research area requires attention to viewpoints that are held by a large portion of the population and that exert significant influence on policy or society, it would be advantageous to have someone on faculty who either holds the view or conducts research on those who do. More specifically, when such viewpoints concern values, or concern matters on which there is not scholarly consensus, it would be advantageous to have a faculty member who holds the view; in contrast, when there is evidence-based scholarly consensus that the relevant view is false, it would be advantageous to have someone who studies those who hold that view.

Universities should thus try particularly hard to hire faculty who hold disfavored or controversial views when those views are held by a large portion of the population, have not been clearly refuted, and influence culture and policy.

Application of this principle to topics and viewpoints that are currently underrepresented in academic work would both preserve disciplinary autonomy and scholarly standards and also increase viewpoint diversity in ways that enhance the pursuit of knowledge.

If this principle were applied consistently, I could imagine faculty searches being conducted in sociology or in public health on marriage and health; in psychology, on character and virtue assessment; in philosophy, on Thomas Aquinas, whose philosophy (not just theology) continues to exert major influence on the Catholic Church and its 1.4 billion adherents. More controversially, a school of public health might consider hiring a pro-life scholar of women's health.

Hires in these often-neglected areas would increase the political, intellectual, and religious diversity of the faculty. Adding scholars with different perspectives might allow us to find some common ground on divisive issues. It would certainly improve the quality of argument and scholarship on both sides.

That many would consider such a proposal objectionable may itself be evidence that ideological factors often drive faculty hiring.

To be clear, not all widely held viewpoints deserve equal consideration under this principle. Many believe in alien UFOs, but this does not exert major policy influence. While numerous Americans embrace young-earth creationist views, which exert some societal influence, there is scholarly consensus against the position. However, having a scholar who studies those holding such views would likely give a department a strong advantage in the transmission of knowledge.

Greater viewpoint diversity would produce a host of positive follow-on effects. It would reshape what are central versus fringe topics within a discipline, and editorial willingness to publish on them in high-ranked journals. This may in turn affect who is hired and promoted.

Likewise, a lack of viewpoint diversity among faculty also affects graduate students. It is difficult for graduate students to study certain topics if they can't find faculty to advise them. Without faculty interested in unfashionable topics, prospective students may decide it isn't worth applying or may face rejection for lack of advisors. In turn, the absence of graduate students studying these subjects reinforces a perception that departments don't need to hire in these areas.

Expanded viewpoint diversity would ultimately serve the University's pursuit of Veritas, in helping us refine, strengthen, correct, and appropriately situate our arguments, as we encounter those with whom we disagree.

Harvard scholars and leadership would do well to recall Richard Feynman's wise words: "The first principle is that you must not fool yourself—and you are the easiest person to fool."

Law Schools Must Create a Culture That Promotes Viewpoint Diversity—Here's How

by Keith J. Hand and Komi Frey

(originally published in *Minding the Campus* on August 30, 2024)

In June 2024, more than one hundred deans signed a joint letter calling for law schools to support constitutional democracy by teaching students to disagree respectfully and engage across ideological divides.[1] As around forty thousand new law students begin their professional education this fall, it is fair to question whether law schools have demonstrated a commitment to this principle in practice. To ensure that law students graduate with an understanding of a full range of perspectives on complex legal issues, law schools must actively expose students to diverse viewpoints, particularly those that challenge progressive orthodoxy in the legal academy. Yet many law students lack meaningful opportunities to interact with conservative or originalist lawyers, scholars, and jurists during their legal education.

Why does this matter? As of August 2024, nearly half of all federal judges and more than half of federal appellate judges were appointed by Republican presidents. How well will law graduates

This essay has been lightly revised to accommodate the print format of the volume.

present their cases to such judges if they cannot even allow them to speak, as we witnessed when Judge Kyle Duncan visited Stanford Law School in 2023? And what about ideologically diverse clients and jurors? Over a third of Americans identify as politically conservative.[2] Will law graduates provide quality legal representation to these Americans? Will they develop the skills to persuade ideologically diverse juries? Or will they heckle those who have, as Yale Law School students did at an ideologically diverse panel on expression rights in 2022?

Law schools shouldn't get a pass for issuing aspirational statements while perpetuating inquiry-stifling norms. To assess a law school's commitment to engagement across ideological divides in practice, faculty, students, and alumni should ask hard questions about the following six institutional characteristics: the ideological composition of the faculty; the law school's commitment to institutional neutrality; the ideological diversity of invited speakers, institutional events, and institutional media; the clarity of institutional commitments to free inquiry; and whether administrators defend faculty when they are targeted for their expression. We discuss each below.

Is there meaningful ideological diversity among the law school faculty?

A recent national study found that only 15 percent of law faculty identify as conservative.[3] The percentage is even lower at many leading law schools in progressive regions. And, as one comprehensive study of self-censorship among faculty revealed, seven in ten right-leaning academics in the social sciences and humanities self-censor and report a hostile climate, compared to only four in ten left-leaning faculty.[4] Consequently, the views of conservative faculty may be heard even less often than one might expect based on their national representation.

Why should this matter, even to progressive law professors and administrators? Ideologically homogeneous groups are prone to pluralistic ignorance, groupthink, group polarization, and preference falsification. These phenomena occur when individuals refrain from dissent for fear of social rejection or group dissolution. Consequently, groups may rush important decisions, fail to assess alternatives, and prescribe ineffective solutions to problems they do not fully understand.

These dynamics undermine the quality of legal education and scholarship. If legal professionals only engage with like-minded colleagues, they may fail to anticipate and truly understand opposing arguments, to the detriment of client interests. To address this problem, law schools should expose students to legal arguments that diverge from dominant perspectives at the school. These arguments should be presented by scholars who actually believe them to ensure that law students grapple with the strongest defenses of such positions.

Has the law school committed to institutional neutrality?

In recent years, law school deans have issued biased statements on many political and legal matters, including the 2016 election, Trump's immigration policies, the Russia-Ukraine war, and Supreme Court decisions on abortion and affirmative action. When deans convey institutional stances on complex disputes, they chill the expression of dissenting viewpoints and undermine the core duty of the university. As the 1967 Kalven Report on institutional neutrality explains, this duty is to "sustain an extraordinary environment of freedom of inquiry and maintain an independence from political fashions, passions, and pressures."[5]

The correct institutional response to major political events is to refrain from issuing any statements at all. At least 148 institutions have taken steps in this direction by adopting some form of institutional neutrality.[6] If institutions formally adopt statements on institutional neutrality, as leading advocates for open inquiry recommend, administrators can cite their logic when pressure campaigns surface.[7]

Does the law school sponsor and promote viewpoint-diverse events and speakers?

Most law schools organize a wide range of institutional events. How often are legal experts featured because their perspectives diverge from dominant ideologies at the law school? Law schools must do more than simply honor their legal obligations to tolerate Federalist Society events. We agree with Eugene Volokh, who argues that law schools should proactively organize discussions of controversial topics themselves.[8] For example, at George Mason University, Voices for Liberty hosted a "Discussion over Division" event in early 2024 where participants were "matched with students of differing political views for engaging conversations." Progressive students should have opportunities to understand ideological counterparts and sharpen arguments through robust debate with legal experts who think differently, just as their conservative classmates do.

Does the law school promote diverse viewpoints in its institutional media?

Institutional communications create and reinforce norms. When browsing a law school's website or social media, are a range of views represented disinterestedly, or are certain viewpoints favored? Keith reviewed the institutional Facebook feed of his home institution, the University of California College of the Law, San Francisco. Of hundreds of posts during the 2023–2024 academic year, around a third exhibited a progressive ideological slant, while none had a conservative or libertarian slant. Of course, institutions committed to viewpoint diversity should include progressive views. But a dramatic imbalance chills expression by signaling institutional preferences for certain viewpoints. And, because institutions have an interest in promoting their own events and faculty, such imbalances are a strong indication of problems with viewpoint diversity throughout the institution.

Do law school statements and training clearly commit to academic freedom and freedom of expression?

Most law schools have legal obligations to train community members on unlawful discrimination or harassment. Such training is appropriate and necessary. However, some programs also incorporate lessons that caution against legitimate expression that others might find insensitive. This can leave even law faculty uncertain about the line between protected expression and actionable harassment. Because the potential costs of disciplinary proceedings are so high, students and faculty may err on the side of silence.

To offer reassurance, law schools ought to formally adopt policies that echo the Chicago Statement: "[C]oncerns about civility and mutual respect can never be used as a justification for closing off discussion of ideas, however offensive or disagreeable those ideas may be to some members of our community."[9] In addition, all students and faculty should receive instruction on academic freedom and expression rights. Institutions such as the University of California National Center for Free Speech and Engagement provide resources on free expression to promote such instruction.[10]

How does your law school respond to attempts to sanction scholars or speakers?

Law professors are targeted for cancellation more often than professors in any other discipline. The Foundation for Individual Rights and Expression's Scholars Under Fire database reveals that from 2000 to early 2024, there were at least 110 attempts to professionally sanction law professors for speech that is, or in public settings would be, protected by the First Amendment. Over half of the sanction attempts in that sample (62 out of 110; 56 percent) occurred from 2020 to 2024. This uptick was largely due to growing intolerance among people on the Left, who initiated over 70 percent of those attempts (44 out of 62; 71 percent). In this climate, some law faculty simply avoid discussing sensitive cases or controversial arguments germane to their fields, for fear of triggering complaints.[11] And such fear is understandable, as too many attempts to sanction law professors succeed. Nearly 60 percent of attempts (64 out of 110; 58 percent) resulted in some form of sanction. Even if faculty are cleared, they may endure costly administrative investigations and reputational harm.

While every cancellation attempt chills expression, we highlight four egregious examples here:

- In a 2023 incident at Brigham Young University, law students in the American Constitution Society successfully pressured the administration to cancel a Federalist Society event. Nebraska College of Law professor Rick Duncan and BYU Law professor Fred Gedicts were scheduled to debate the Supreme Court's decision in *Dobbs Jackson Women's Health Organization*, the case that overturned *Roe* v. *Wade*. Students opposed Duncan's invitation because he'd previously argued that requiring the use of preferred pronouns constitutes compelled speech.
- At George Washington University, students penned an open letter in 2022 demanding Supreme Court Justice Clarence Thomas's removal from teaching in the wake of his concurring opinion in *Dobbs*. To their credit, administrators did not bow to this pressure. However, a month after the cancellation campaign began, Thomas claimed that he was no longer available to teach the course.
- At Harvard University, students demanded that law professor Ronald Sullivan Jr. resign as faculty dean of Winthrop House in 2019 because he joined Harvey Weinstein's legal defense team and expressed concerns about the investigation of economics professor Roland Fryer. Although

fifty-two Harvard law professors expressed support for Sullivan's "legal advocacy in service of constitutional principles," the dean of Harvard College refused to renew the deanships of both Sullivan and his wife, Stephanie Robinson, citing an "untenable environment."

- At the University of Florida, administrators barred law professors Kenneth Nunn and Teresa Jean Reid from signing an amicus brief in a 2020 lawsuit. The suit challenged a state Senate bill requiring felons to pay court-ordered costs before voting. Nunn and Reid were told that opposing the state government was "adverse" to the university's interests. UF faculty filed a lawsuit challenging the policy that allows the university to block them from testifying against the state in legal cases.

Although we have focused primarily on why a deficit of conservative views in law schools should concern lawyers across the ideological spectrum, our last example highlights an emerging threat to progressive viewpoints. As public trust in higher education erodes,[12] conservative politicians have introduced legislation to regulate the teaching of "divisive concepts" or impose viewpoint diversity requirements. Even if courts block the most egregious legislation on constitutional grounds, procedures such as post-tenure review may pass. Such state legislation undermines the ability of progressive scholars to teach and research. Law schools can preempt inquiry-stifling state intervention by promoting viewpoint diversity themselves.

As the American Bar Association observed in adopting a new accreditation standard on academic freedom in February 2024, the "free, robust, and uninhibited sharing of ideas reflecting a wide range of viewpoints" is essential to an effective legal education.[13] To advance this core objective in practice, law schools must take more proactive steps to ensure the presentation of ideologically diverse views and curb implicit institutional signals that stifle such exchange. The quality of tomorrow's legal minds and our civic discourse depend on it.

Notes

1 Letter from the Deans of American Law School, June 18, 2024, https://www.americanbar.org/content/dam/aba/administrative/news/2024/deans-letter-061824.pdf.

2 Lydia Saad, "U.S. Political Ideology Steady; Conservatives, Moderates Tie," Gallup, January 17, 2022, https://news.gallup.com/poll/388988/political-ideology-steady-conservatives-moderates-tie.aspx.

3 Adam Bonica, Adam Chilton, Kyle Rozema, and Maya Sen, "The Legal Academy's Ideological Uniformity," *The Journal of Legal Studies* 47, no. 1 (January 2018): 3.

4 Eric Kaufman, *Academic Freedom in Crisis: Punishment, Political Discrimination, and Self-Censorship*, Center for the Study of Partisanship and Ideology Report No. 2., March 1, 2021, https://www.cspicenter.com/p/academic-freedom-in-crisis-punishment.

5 Kalven Committee, *Report on the University's Role in Political and Social Action*, The University of Chicago, November 11, 1967, https://provost.uchicago.edu/sites/default/files/documents/reports/KalvenRprt_0.pdf.

6 Alex Arnold, Erin Shaw, Nate Tenhundfeld, and Nicole Barbaro, *The Rising Tide of Statement Neutrality in Higher Education: How Universities are Rethinking Institutional Speech*, Heterodox Academy, March 2025, https://content.heterodoxacademy.org/uploads/HxA_Statement-Neutrality-Report_FINAL.pdf.

7 Academic Freedom Alliance, Heterodox Academy, FIRE, Joint Statement: College and University Trustees and Regents Must Join Peers in Committing to Institutional Neutrality, July 11, 2024, https://institutionalneutrality.org.

8 Eugene Volokh, "Free Speech Rules, Free Speech Culture, and Legal Education," *Hofstra Law Review* 51, no. 3 (2023): 645–649.

9 *Report of the Committee of Freedom of Expression at the University of Chicago*, January 2015, https://provost.uchicago.edu/sites/default/files/documents/reports/FOECommitteeReport.pdf.

10 "First Amendment/Freedom of Expression Education Resources," University of California National Center for Free Speech and Civic Engagement, accessed August 27, 2025, https://freespeechcenter.university

ofcalifornia.edu/programs-and-resources/resource-materials/first-amendment-freedom-of-expression-resources/.

11 Aaron Sibarium, "The Takeover of America's Legal System," *The Free Press*, March 21, 2022, https://www.thefp.com/p/the-takeover-of-americas-legal-system?s=r.

12 Megan Brenan, "Americans' Confidence in Higher Education Down Sharply," Gallup, July 11, 2023, https://news.gallup.com/poll/508352/americans-confidence-higher-education-down-sharply.aspx.

13 American Bar Association Section of Legal Education and Admissions to the Bar Revised Standards for Approval of Law Schools, February 2024, https://www.americanbar.org/content/dam/aba/directories/policy/midyear-2024/300-midyear-2024.pdf.

Unfinished Business: Viewpoint Diversity and the Culture of Teaching

by Jonathan Zimmerman

In an April 2025 letter to Harvard University, the Trump administration ordered the school to ensure that all its departments were "viewpoint diverse."[1] That earned a stinging rebuke from Harvard president Alan Garber, who said the order violated long-standing norms of academic freedom. But Garber also admitted that the university had not always abided by its proclaimed values of full and robust debate across ideological differences. "We acknowledge that we have unfinished business," Garber wrote. "We need to ensure that the university lives up to its steps to reaffirm a culture of free inquiry, viewpoint diversity, and academic exploration."[2]

Here's what he didn't say: Harvard needs to teach better.

That's the *real* unfinished business of higher education. When a recent survey asked Americans what makes the "best" college or university, the most common response was "It has professors who are excellent teachers." Yet most colleges and universities have failed to prepare faculty members for the classroom or to evaluate them in a meaningful way. Most of all, we have incentivized research over teaching. At every type of institution, from small community colleges to huge private and state universities, professors who devote the most time to research receive the highest salaries; meanwhile, faculty who expend more effort on their instruction earn less.[3] In short, we have not valued teaching as a professional endeavor or responsibility.

So, what does that have to do with viewpoint diversity?

A lot. As a growing body of evidence suggests, the best teaching engages students in their own learning.[4] They don't simply imbibe information and regurgitate it on papers and exams; instead, they address the urgent questions of their disciplines and formulate their own answers. That won't work if we all think the same way.

And it certainly won't work if we don't care much about teaching—or learning—in the first place. If you're not deeply invested in the intellectual formation of your students, you're more likely to give them the "right" answers instead of requiring them to puzzle things out for themselves. "When viewpoint diversity is absent, the classroom environment is negatively affected," Ilana Redstone and John Villasenor underlined in their book, *Unassailable Ideas*.[5]

They're right. But where concern about the classroom environment is absent, viewpoint diversity won't matter. Of course we should challenge our students with multiple perspectives and theories. Yet that will require a commitment to teaching that is too often missing from the American university. The most unassailable idea—which we all need to counter—is that our institutions recognize and reward high-quality instruction. They don't.

Sure, they provide a range of teaching prizes. But everyone knows that you can make more money by publishing another book or article—and getting promoted to a higher salary rank—than by winning a one-off teaching award. These prizes date to the 1960s and 1970s, when student protesters like Mario Savio and Tom Hayden denounced professors who buried themselves in the library or laboratory at the expense of the classroom. In response, dozens of universities started to offer teaching prizes. But several early winners at Stanford and other elite schools were denied tenure because they didn't publish enough, which confirmed the larger truth: Research was still king.[6]

Several years ago, when I was working at New York University, I was fortunate enough to win its Distinguished Teaching Award. When my dean—who was also a friend—came to the podium to introduce me, she read a list of the books I had written! I don't begrudge her for that, at all. What else did she have to go on, really? At NYU, where I taught for twenty years, I was observed in the classroom exactly once—during my first semester there—by my department chair. I'm now in my ninth year at Penn, and nobody with any supervisory authority has ever come to watch me teach. I could be doing anything. Or nothing.

To be sure, my students fill out evaluation surveys about me every term. But very few people—students, faculty, or administrators—take these reports seriously. One student told me she regards them like those annoying emails you receive after a trip, asking you to comment on the plane ride or the hotel. I appreciate students who complete the evaluations carefully and—especially—those who provide me with suggestions for improving my courses. But they're in the minority. Likewise, most administrators don't put a lot of faith or credit in student evaluations. The reports are subject to all the biases and prejudices in our society: men get ranked more highly than women, whites get better marks than non-whites, and so on. And there's also evidence that student evaluations contribute to grade inflation.[7] If you want a more positive report from your students, hand out more A's. They'll like you.

Let me be clear: There are some excellent teachers at our universities. There are also some terrible teachers, and a whole lot in between. The problem is that we don't make a consistent or substantive effort to figure out which is which. When I finished writing a history of college teaching in the United States, I didn't submit it to a group of undergraduates to see if it had anything interesting to say. I sent it instead to several scholars who had spent their careers examining the history and politics of the

American university. If we took teaching seriously, it would be peer-reviewed—just like our research. And we would also check to see if our classroom instruction corresponded to the research about teaching. I entitled my book *The Amateur Hour* not because all professors teach poorly—again, only some of them do—but rather because we haven't developed systems to judge whether their instruction follows best practices. That's what professions do: They regulate themselves in accord with the knowledge they have generated. And while universities have professionalized their research function (see: peer review), teaching remains an amateur endeavor.

If we made a good-faith effort to bolster teaching, we would almost surely broaden the expression of diverse viewpoints as well. The best teachers assign readings from a range of political perspectives, so students encounter ideas that diverge from their own. And, most of all, effective teachers make explicit and concerted efforts to draw out different opinions in the classroom. That means laying down very clear guidelines for discussion, starting with my own favorite teaching rule: critique the speech, not the speaker. So, if someone says something that you think is unwise or false, I tell my students, don't call them stupid or uninformed: that's a formula for muzzling conversation rather than enhancing it. Ask instead why they think what they think—that is, what evidence they have for their claim—or introduce other information that points to a different conclusion. Second, emphasize that students will be evaluated based on the quality of their arguments—including, again, their evidence—rather than on whether they agree with their professor. All teachers must decide how much of their own perspective to divulge in class: doing so risks tilting the discussion in your favor, but maintaining a neutral poise can seem inauthentic or contrived. (And the students can often see right through it.) But if you choose to share your views, you must make it absolutely clear that nobody else in the room is required to agree with them.

Every month brings a new survey demonstrating that students—especially those of a conservative bent—are afraid to say what they think, particularly when it diverges from their left-leaning professors. We can't solve that problem simply by hiring more conservative faculty members. If our professors—whatever their politics—don't have the incentive or ability to teach well, they won't foster the rigorous inquiry and dialogue that real education demands. Nor will they harness viewpoint diversity on campus, where there is a wider array of opinion than many of us imagine. At Penn, for example, 12 percent of undergraduates surveyed in October 2024 said they planned to vote for Donald Trump in the November elections.[8] That's a small fraction, but Penn is a big place: We have over ten thousand undergrads, so over a thousand of them favored Trump. But they're mostly in the closet—as one of my Trump-friendly students quipped—because they don't want to be canceled by their peers. Any teacher worth their salt would try to elicit these voices in class so everyone else could learn from them. And, most of all, an effective teacher would demonstrate the skills that we all need to converse across our differences: reason, humility, and tolerance. These virtues are essential to democracy, but they're not "natural"; they are learned, by example and practice. If we don't model them in our classrooms, our students won't acquire them.

I recognize that these dialogues are more likely to take place in a philosophy or politics class than in, say, chemistry or physics. And I also know that there are some professors—especially those on the progressive Left—who simply want right-leaning students to keep quiet. Others might fear introducing anything controversial because they worry about losing control of the class; still others fret about getting poor marks from offended students on course evaluations, which have often asked about the professor's "sensitivity" around racial and ethnic (not ideological) diversity.[9] But the most common inhibitor is the one we talk the least about: an overall lack of investment in teaching. A professor who was well-prepared for that task would know how to address contentious issues in class; even more, she or he would *want* to explore them, because exposure to different points of view helps students learn.

Leading such discussions isn't a "natural" skill, either; you need a systematic induction into it. That means learning how to seize upon the "teachable moments" when controversial questions arise; how to encourage people to speak up when they are reluctant to do so; how to gently correct students when they say something disrespectful to their peers; and how to bring a discussion to a close when it becomes dull or repetitive. To get a PhD at my university, you must produce a piece of original research that might take as long as ten years to research and write. But to become a teaching assistant, you take a three-day seminar on pedagogy. That's better than nothing—and it's more than some other schools require—but it speaks volumes about what we really value. I play tennis, not squash; I would need a lot of instruction and practice in the latter sport before I could feel comfortable competing in it. But we still put professors with almost no teaching knowledge or experience in front of roomfuls of students, which is a lot like putting me on a squash court: It's a formula for failure. Borrowing a different metaphor, Rice University literature professor George C. Williams observed back in 1958 that a new college teacher was like a pilot who takes off without knowing how to fly. "Tragedy for the pilot is almost inevitable; in the case of the young instructor, the tragedy befalls his students," Williams wrote.[10]

In fairness, the overall quality of classroom instruction has almost surely improved since Williams's time.[11] But it's not good enough. In a close study of 732 instructors at nine institutions over ten years, American University education scholar Corbin Campbell found that the best teaching, on average, occurs in regional state universities and small liberal arts colleges; the worst happens at big research universities, like the ones where I have spent my career.[12] But we won't have much incentive to get better until someone holds our feet to the fire. What if *U.S. News and World Report*—or some other enterprise—produced a ranking of colleges and universities based on their quality of instruction? *U.S. News* already reports faculty salaries, student-professor ratios, and the average number of dollars spent on each student. But none of those measures is a good proxy for teaching quality; a well-paid professor might have risen to the top by prioritizing research over instruction, for example, and a high-spending university might devote its money to building fancy new gyms and dormitories instead of to providing good teaching. We need more research, like Campbell's, to determine where good—and bad—teaching is taking place. And, most of all, we need to publicize the results so that students and their families can choose schools accordingly. They tell us that they want great teaching, but they have no way of knowing where they can obtain it. A new ranking system would help them find out.

Just as the elite schools score poorly on the free-speech index compiled by the Foundation for Individual Rights and Expression (FIRE), so would many of them cluster near the bottom rung of any new teaching ladder that we created.[13] A school with strong teachers will bring students of different opinions into conversation with each other. But if a school has weak instruction, it's much less likely to spawn that kind of dialogue. To be sure, the college classroom is not the only determinant of campus culture around viewpoint diversity. But it is the one the faculty members can influence—for good or ill—because they are in charge of it. We can't change how students interact in the dorms or on the quad. We can affect what they do in class, but only—again—if we care about their learning, and if we have the skills to engage them in it.

That brings us back to the epic battle between the Trump administration and Harvard. You can trace its roots to the disastrous Congressional appearance of university president Claudine

Gay in December 2023, a year before Trump was returned to the White House. Gay testified two months after Hamas attacked Israel, which triggered a full-scale invasion of Gaza and—in turn—loud anti-Israel protests on American campuses. Most of the media reports about the hearing focused on Gay's reply to the "gotcha" question by Rep. Elise Stefanik (R-NY), who asked if calling for the genocide of Jews would be allowed on campus; Gay said yes, because the university depends on the free and open exchange of ideas. Much less noticed was Gay's response to Rep. Virginia Foxx (R-NC), who asked whether Harvard faculty were prepared for that kind of give-and-take in the classroom. "To be a successful teacher and educator at Harvard requires the ability to draw out all of the viewpoints and voices in your classroom, irrespective of one's political views," Gay declared. "And we devote significant resources to training our faculty in that pedagogical skill and prioritizing that in our recruiting and hiring."[14]

Gay was right, about what it takes to be a good teacher. But I would wager good money that Harvard doesn't spend a king's ransom on preparing faculty to teach; I also doubt that "pedagogical skill" enters heavily into its hiring decisions. And if the university was really making good on the promise of viewpoint diversity, it would look and feel very different than it does today. "You could imagine a campus that's really diverse, but nobody talks to each other," said philosopher Ned Hall, the co-president of the university's Council on Academic Freedom, following the Trump administration's attacks in 2025. "What we really, really, really need is a campus intellectual culture that makes use of that diversity."[15] Hall was right, too. Changing that culture starts with better teaching. Indeed, it's hard to imagine any useful change that doesn't.

Notes

1 Josh Greunbaum et al. to Alan M. Garber and Penny Pritzker, April 11, 2025, https://www.thecrimson.com/widget/2025/4/15/demands-letter-to-harvard/.

2 Alan Garber, "Upholding Our Values, Defending Our University," Harvard University Office of the President, April 21, 2025: https://www.harvard.edu/president/news/2025/upholding-our-values-defending-our-university/.

3 Corbin Campbell, *Great College Teaching: Where It Happens and How to Foster It Everywhere*, with Jonathan Gyurko (Cambridge: Harvard Education Press, 2023), 48–49; James S. Fairweather, "Faculty Reward Structures: Toward Institutional and Professional Homogenization," *Research in Higher Education* 34, no. 5 (1993): 603–23:https://doi.org/10.1007/BF00991922; Harry Brighouse, "Taking Undergraduate Teaching and Learning Seriously," in *Academic Ethics Today: Problems, Policies, and Prospects for University Life*, ed. Steven M Cahn (Lanham: Rowman and Littlefield, 2022), 261–72.

4 For the best summary of this research, see David Gooblar, *The Missing Course: Everything They Never Taught You About College Teaching*, 1st ed. (Cambridge: Harvard University Press, 2021). See also Aaron M. Pallas and Anna Neumann, *Convergent Teaching: Tools to Spark Deeper Learning in College*, Reforming Higher Education: Innovation and the Public Good (Baltimore: Johns Hopkins University Press, 2019); Joshua Eyler, *How Humans Learn: The Science and Stories behind Effective College Teaching*, Teaching and Learning in Higher Education (Morgantown: West Virginia University Press, 2018).

5 Ilana Redstone and John Villasenor, *Unassailable Ideas: How Unwritten Rules and Social Media Shape Discourse in American Higher Education* (New York: Oxford University Press, 2020), 111.

6 Jonathan Zimmerman, *The Amateur Hour: A History of College Teaching in America* (Baltimore: Johns Hopkins University Press, 2020), 161–62, 214–15.

7 See, e.g., Wolfgang Stroebe, "Student Evaluations of Teaching Encourages Poor Teaching and Contributes to Grade Inflation: A Theoretical and Empirical Analysis," *Basic and Applied Social Psychology* 42, no. 4 (2020): 276–94, https://doi.org/10.1080/01973533.2020.1756817.

8 Makenzie Kerneckel, "Harris Overwhelmingly Leads Trump among Penn Students, DP Election Poll Finds," *The Daily Pennsylvanian*, October 28, 2024: https://www.thedp.com/article/2024/10/penn-voter-survey-harris-trump-2024.

9 Zimmerman, *The Amateur Hour*, 228–29.

10 George Williams, *Some of My Best Friends Are Professors: A Critical Commentary on Higher Education* (New York: Abelard-Schuman, 1958), 239.

11 Steven G. Brint, *Two Cheers for Higher Education: Why American Universities Are Stronger Than Ever—And How to Meet the Challenges They Face*, The William G. Bowen Ser, v. 112 (Princeton: Princeton University Press, 2019), 315–24.

12 Campbell, *Great College Teaching*, 120–26.

13 Sean T. Stevens, *2025 College Free Speech Rankings: What Is the State of Free Speech on America's College Campuses?*, FIRE (Foundation for Individual Rights and Expression), 2025.

14 Katherine Knott, "3 Presidents on the Hot Seat," *Inside Higher Ed*, December 5, 2023: https://www.insidehighered.com/news/government/2023/12/05/house-republicans-castigate-presidents-harvard-penn-and-mit.

15 Jennifer Schuessler, "Trump and Harvard Both Want 'Viewpoint Diversity.' What Does It Mean?," *The New York Times*, May 5, 2025: https://www.nytimes.com/2025/05/05/arts/harvard-trump-viewpoint-diversity.html.

Counterpoints: An Effective Approach to Teaching Viewpoint Diversity

by Nafees Alam

Picture a classroom where every student nods in agreement, where discussions flow smoothly because everyone shares the same perspective, and where the professor's viewpoints are accepted without question. On the surface, this might seem like an ideal learning environment: peaceful, harmonious, and efficient. But what if I told you this classroom is actually failing its students in the most fundamental way possible?

This is the reality in many educational settings today, where the goal has subtly shifted from teaching students how to think to telling them what to think. It's a comfortable arrangement for everyone involved. Professors don't have to defend their positions, students don't have to grapple with uncomfortable ideas, and everyone leaves feeling validated in their existing beliefs. But comfort and education are often at odds with each other.

The Point-Counterpoint approach to teaching offers a radically different vision of education, one that embraces intellectual diversity, celebrates disagreement, and transforms classrooms into laboratories for critical thinking. At its core, this methodology rests on a simple but powerful principle: for every perspective, there exists an equally valid counter-perspective that deserves examination. Understanding any issue requires engaging seriously with viewpoints that challenge our own.

This approach matters now more than ever. We live in an era of increasing polarization, where people retreat into echo chambers that reinforce their existing beliefs. Social media algorithms feed us content that aligns with our preferences, news outlets cater to specific ideological audiences, and even our social circles often consist of like-minded individuals. In this context, the classroom may be one of the last spaces where people can encounter genuinely diverse perspectives in a structured, supportive environment.

The Mathematics of Thought

To understand why viewpoint diversity matters in education, consider an analogy from mathematics. In differential equations, there are two types of solutions: null solutions and particular solutions. The null solution represents a state where all variables converge to zero—a uniform, stable, but ultimately lifeless equilibrium. The particular solution, on the other hand, embraces complexity and variation, producing rich, dynamic outcomes that reflect real-world conditions.

It's easier to manage a classroom where everyone thinks alike. But this simplicity comes at a tremendous cost: An education system that prioritizes intellectual uniformity fails to prepare students for a world characterized by diversity, disagreement, and constant change.

The particular solution presented here, with all its openness to change and complexity, offers a better model for education. It acknowledges that different starting points lead to different outcomes, that multiple valid approaches exist for solving problems, and that the interplay between diverse perspectives often produces the most innovative solutions. This is the principle that underlies the Point-Counterpoint approach: Education should embrace intellectual diversity as a feature, not a bug.

Breaking the Bias Barrier

One of the biggest obstacles to viewpoint diversity in education is confirmation bias—our natural tendency to seek out information that confirms what we already believe while avoiding information that challenges our assumptions. This bias affects everyone, from first-year students to tenured professors. In fact, educators may be particularly susceptible because they've spent years developing expertise in their fields, making it harder to acknowledge alternative perspectives.

I've seen this play out countless times in my own teaching. A professor presents a controversial topic, income inequality, for example, and unconsciously frames the discussion in a way that favors their preferred explanation. They might emphasize structural factors if they lean left, or individual responsibility if they lean right. Students pick up on these cues and learn to parrot back the "correct" perspective, not because they've critically evaluated the evidence, but because they want to succeed in the class.

The Point-Counterpoint approach directly confronts this tendency by making bias visible and discussable. Instead of pretending to be neutral arbiters of truth, educators acknowledge their own perspectives while actively introducing competing viewpoints. They might say, "Here's how I tend to think about this issue, but let's explore three alternative frameworks that can lead to different conclusions." This transparency helps students recognize that knowledge is often perspectival and that understanding requires engaging with multiple viewpoints.

Students also bring their own biases to the classroom, often without realizing it. They've been shaped by their families, communities, media consumption, and personal experiences. When confronted with ideas that challenge their worldview, their first instinct is often to dismiss or attack rather than engage. The Point-Counterpoint approach helps students recognize these defensive reactions and develop the intellectual humility to say,

"Maybe there's something here I need to understand, even if I ultimately disagree."

The Art of Productive Disagreement

Perhaps the most radical aspect of the Point-Counterpoint Methodology is its approach to disagreement. In many educational settings, disagreement is seen as a problem to be solved or avoided. Students learn to keep controversial opinions to themselves, to hedge their statements with qualifiers, or to simply echo whatever seems safest. This creates an atmosphere of intellectual timidity that stunts growth and learning.

The Point-Counterpoint approach flips this dynamic by treating disagreement as a valuable educational resource. When students disagree, it's not a failure of teaching; it's an opportunity for deeper learning. The key is creating a framework where viewpoint diversity can be productive rather than destructive.

This starts with establishing ground rules that separate ideas from identity. Students learn to critique arguments without attacking the people making them. They practice saying "I disagree with that interpretation because . . ." rather than "You're wrong." They learn to acknowledge the strengths in opposing arguments before identifying weaknesses. Most importantly, they learn that changing one's mind in light of new evidence or better arguments is a sign of intellectual strength, not weakness.

I remember a particularly heated classroom discussion about criminal justice reform. Students were deeply divided, with some advocating for rehabilitation-focused approaches and others emphasizing punishment and deterrence. Instead of trying to find a comfortable middle ground or shutting down the debate, we leaned into the disagreement. Each side was challenged to articulate the strongest version of the opposing argument before critiquing it. Students had to identify the values and assumptions underlying each position and explore how different life experiences might lead reasonable people to different conclusions.

The discussion was uncomfortable at times, but it was also transformative. Students reported that they left class still disagreeing on many points, but with a much deeper understanding of the complexity of the issue and greater respect for those who thought differently. This is the goal of the Point-Counterpoint approach: not consensus, but understanding.

Beyond Binary Thinking

One of the most valuable outcomes of embracing viewpoint diversity is that it helps students move beyond simplistic, binary thinking. In our polarized age, issues are often framed as having only two sides—you're either for or against, right or wrong, with us or against us. This framing makes for compelling headlines and social media posts, but it rarely captures the full complexity of important issues.

The Point-Counterpoint approach reveals that most significant questions have multiple perspectives, each highlighting different aspects of the issue. Take a seemingly straightforward topic like raising the minimum wage. The binary framing presents it as a choice between helping workers and hurting businesses. But a Point-Counterpoint exploration might examine perspectives from labor economists, small business owners, workers in different industries, economic historians, and policy makers from countries with different approaches. Each perspective adds nuance and complexity, revealing trade-offs and unintended consequences that simple pro/con framings miss.

This multiperspectival approach doesn't lead to relativism or the conclusion that all viewpoints are equally valid. Instead, it helps students develop more sophisticated criteria for evaluating different positions. They learn to ask questions like: What evidence supports this view? What values does it prioritize? What are its logical implications? Who benefits and who might be harmed? By engaging with multiple perspectives, students develop the ability to synthesize insights from different viewpoints and craft more nuanced, defensible positions of their own.

Creating Brave Spaces

Implementing the Point-Counterpoint approach requires rethinking the classroom environment. The trendy concept of "safe spaces" in education, while well-intentioned, can sometimes work against viewpoint diversity by prioritizing comfort over growth. The Point-Counterpoint Methodology advocates for "brave spaces"—environments where students feel supported enough to take intellectual risks and engage with challenging ideas.

A brave space acknowledges that learning often involves discomfort. When our assumptions are challenged, when we realize we've been wrong about something important, when we have to defend our positions against smart criticism, these moments don't feel safe. They feel vulnerable and uncertain. But they're also where the most significant learning happens.

Creating such spaces requires careful attention to both structure and culture. Structurally, it means designing discussions and assignments that explicitly require engagement with multiple viewpoints. Instead of traditional essays arguing for a single position, students might write dialogues between different perspectives or analyze how the same evidence can support different conclusions. Group projects might require teams to include members with different viewpoints and find ways to integrate their perspectives.

Culturally, it means modeling intellectual humility and curiosity. When educators admit uncertainty, acknowledge when they've changed their minds, and genuinely engage with student perspectives that differ from their own, they create permission for students to do the same. It means celebrating moments when students say, "I never thought of it that way before," or "I need to reconsider my position."

The Skills to Practice Viewpoint Diversity

Engaging effectively with diverse viewpoints isn't intuitive; it requires a set of skills that must be developed through practice.

The Point-Counterpoint approach helps students build these essential capacities:

Perspective-taking is perhaps the foundational skill. This goes beyond simply acknowledging that others see things differently. It requires the ability to inhabit different world-views temporarily, to understand not just what others believe but why those beliefs make sense from their standpoint. Students practice this by role-playing different positions in debates, writing from perspectives they don't share, and exploring how different life experiences shape different viewpoints.

Intellectual humility involves recognizing the limitations of one's own knowledge and remaining open to learning from others. This doesn't mean being wishy-washy or lacking conviction. Instead, it means holding one's views with appropriate confidence: strongly when well-supported by evidence and reasoning, more tentatively when based on limited information or personal preference.

Critical empathy combines analytical thinking with emotional intelligence. It's the ability to understand why someone holds a particular view while maintaining the capacity to evaluate that view critically. This prevents both uncritical acceptance of all viewpoints and dismissive rejection of unfamiliar ideas.

Constructive dialogue skills enable students to engage in conversations that deepen understanding rather than deepening divisions. This includes active listening, asking clarifying questions, finding common ground, and disagreeing respectfully. Students learn to navigate the tension between advocating for their own views and remaining genuinely open to other perspectives.

Real-World Applications

The value of the Point-Counterpoint approach extends far beyond the classroom. In professional settings, the ability to understand and integrate diverse viewpoints is increasingly recognized as essential for innovation and problem-solving. Companies that embrace cognitive diversity—different ways of thinking and approaching problems—consistently outperform those that prioritize uniformity.

Consider how this plays out in different fields. In medicine, understanding how patients from different cultural backgrounds think about health and illness leads to more effective treatment. In business, teams that can see products and services from multiple customer perspectives create better solutions. In technology, diverse development teams are better at anticipating how different users will interact with their products and identifying potential problems before they arise.

The Point-Counterpoint approach prepares students for this multiperspectival world by making viewpoint diversity a habit of mind. They learn to automatically ask, "Who else might see this differently?" and "What am I missing?" These questions become particularly valuable when working in diverse teams or serving diverse populations.

Overcoming Resistance

Despite its benefits, the Point-Counterpoint approach often faces resistance from both educators and students. Understanding and addressing this resistance is crucial for successful implementation.

Educators may resist because it requires giving up some control over classroom narratives. It's comfortable to be the expert whose views are accepted without question. Introducing multiple perspectives means acknowledging that one's own viewpoint is just one among potentially many, that expertise doesn't equal omniscience, and that students might sometimes have insights that challenge professorial assumptions. This vulnerability can be uncomfortable, especially for educators who tie their identity closely to their expertise.

There's also the practical challenge of preparation. It's much easier to prepare a lecture presenting one coherent narrative than to research and fairly present multiple perspectives on complex issues. The Point-Counterpoint approach requires educators to step outside their comfort zones, engaging seriously with viewpoints they might personally find objectionable or wrong-headed.

Students may resist for different reasons. Many come to education seeking answers, not more questions. They want to know the "right" way to think about issues, especially those that will be on the test. The Point-Counterpoint approach's emphasis on complexity and multiple valid perspectives can be frustrating for students who prefer clear-cut answers.

There's also the emotional challenge. Engaging with viewpoints that challenge deeply held beliefs can be genuinely distressing. A student whose family has been harmed by a particular policy might struggle to dispassionately analyze arguments in favor of that policy. A student with strong religious convictions might find it difficult to engage with secular perspectives on moral issues.

Overcoming this resistance requires patience, transparency, and support. Educators need to explain why they're using this approach and how it benefits students in the long run. They need to acknowledge the difficulty while maintaining high expectations. Most importantly, they need to create structures that support students through the challenge—peer discussion groups, reflective writing assignments, and opportunities to process emotional responses to difficult material.

The Transformation of Understanding

When successfully implemented, the Point-Counterpoint approach transforms not just what students know but how they understand knowledge itself. They move from seeing education as the accumulation of correct answers to understanding it as the development of intellectual tools for navigating complexity.

This transformation shows up in various ways. Students become more comfortable with ambiguity and uncertainty, recognizing that many important questions don't have simple answers. They develop stronger analytical skills, are able to identify assumptions, evaluate evidence, and trace the logical implications of different positions. Perhaps most importantly, they become more intellectually generous, able to find value in perspectives they don't share and learn from people they disagree with.

I've watched students undergo this transformation countless times. They enter class certain about their views on controversial topics and leave still holding many of the same values, but with a much more nuanced understanding of the issues involved. They report being better able to have productive conversations with family members who think differently, to work effectively with colleagues from different backgrounds, and to adapt their communication style to different audiences.

Building Bridges in a Divided World

As our society becomes increasingly polarized, the need for people who can bridge different perspectives becomes ever more urgent. The Point-Counterpoint approach develops these bridge-builders by teaching students to find connections across differences.

This doesn't mean adopting a false equivalence where all viewpoints are treated as equally valid or searching for a mushy middle ground that satisfies no one. Instead, it means developing the capacity to understand different perspectives well enough to identify shared values, common concerns, and potential areas of cooperation. It means learning to translate between different worldviews, helping people who start from different assumptions find ways to work together on shared problems.

In practice, this might look like students learning to facilitate discussions between people with opposing views on climate policy by helping them identify shared concerns about future generations. Or it might involve finding common ground between different approaches to education reform by focusing on the shared goal of helping all students succeed. These bridging skills become increasingly valuable as students move into careers where they'll need to work with diverse stakeholders to solve complex problems.

The Future of Education

The Point-Counterpoint approach represents more than just a teaching technique—it's a vision for what education could become in an interconnected, diverse world. Instead of institutions that reinforce existing beliefs and deepen social divisions, schools and universities could become laboratories for productive engagement across differences.

Imagine classrooms where students from different backgrounds come together not to be molded into a uniform shape but to learn from and with each other. Where controversial topics are explored rather than avoided. Where disagreement is seen as an opportunity rather than a threat. Where students graduate not just with knowledge but with the skills and dispositions needed to navigate a complex, pluralistic world.

This vision requires courage from educators willing to give up the comfortable authority of having all the answers. It requires institutions willing to support experimentation and accept that real learning sometimes looks messy. Most of all, it requires a fundamental shift in how we think about the purpose of education: from producing graduates who know the right answers to developing citizens who can think critically, engage constructively with difference, and contribute to solving our shared challenges.

A Call to Action

The Point-Counterpoint approach offers a practical path toward achieving viewpoint diversity in education. But realizing its potential requires action at multiple levels.

Individual educators can start small, introducing elements of the approach into their existing courses. This might mean adding readings that challenge the dominant narrative in their field, structuring one discussion using Point-Counterpoint principles, or designing an assignment that requires students to engage with multiple perspectives. The key is to start somewhere and learn from the experience.

Students can advocate for viewpoint diversity in their own education. They can seek out courses and professors who challenge them to think differently, form study groups with peers who have different perspectives, and practice engaging constructively with ideas they find challenging. They can also support classmates who express unpopular views, helping create an environment where intellectual diversity can flourish.

Institutions can create structures and incentives that support viewpoint diversity. This might include professional development programs that help faculty implement approaches like Point-Counterpoint, revision of course evaluation criteria to value intellectual diversity, and creation of spaces and programs that bring together students from different backgrounds and perspectives.

Parents and community members can support educational approaches that prepare young people for a diverse world rather than demanding that schools reinforce particular viewpoints. They can engage in productive dialogue about education goals and support educators who take the brave step of embracing viewpoint diversity.

Conclusion: The Courage to Understand

At its heart, the Point-Counterpoint approach is about developing the courage to understand perspectives different from our own. This is not the false courage of sticking to our guns regardless of evidence or argument. Nor is it the timidity of never taking a stand. It's the mature courage to hold strong convictions while remaining open to learning, to advocate for our values while respecting those who prioritize different values, and to work for change while acknowledging the complexity of the challenges we face.

In a world that often rewards ideological purity and punishes nuance, this kind of courage is increasingly rare. But it's also increasingly necessary. The challenges we face, from climate change to inequality to technological disruption, require solutions that integrate insights from multiple perspectives. They require people who can work across differences, build unlikely coalitions, and find innovative approaches that transcend traditional divisions.

The Point-Counterpoint approach develops these capacities by making viewpoint diversity not just an ideal but a practice. Every classroom discussion that genuinely engages multiple perspectives, every assignment that requires students to think from different standpoints, every moment when a student says, "I hadn't thought of it that way"—these are small steps toward a more thoughtful, inclusive, and innovative society.

The question is not whether we need viewpoint diversity in education; the evidence for its value is overwhelming. The question is whether we have the courage to embrace it, with all the discomfort and uncertainty it entails. The Point-Counterpoint approach shows that we can create educational environments that honor both intellectual rigor and human dignity, preparing students for life in a complex world.

This is the transformation that awaits when we move from education as agreement to education as understanding. It's challenging, sometimes uncomfortable, and always rewarding. Most importantly, it's necessary if we want to prepare students not just to navigate our divided world but to help heal it. The tools are available, the need is clear, and the time is now. What remains is for us to take the brave step of putting these ideas into practice, one classroom at a time.

Viewpoint Diversity Can Kill Zombie Ideas (or Prevent Them from Arising in the First Place)

by Jesse Singal

Advocates for viewpoint diversity make a simple argument: Intellectual communities benefit from the presence of individuals holding a wide variety of views. This is not as straightforward as ideological diversity—it's not simply about ensuring an approximately equal number of donkeys versus elephants. Rather, it's about accounting for a variety of worldviews and their potentially salutary effects on debate, knowledge production, and the other tasks of intellectual life.

A lack of sufficient viewpoint diversity, such advocates argue, can cause things to go astray. The Implicit Association Test is one example. On May 14, 2025, the American Psychological Association published a blog post titled "The implicit association test: Shining a light on hidden beliefs."[1] The article had the slug BREAKTHROUGH PSYCHOLOGICAL SCIENCE above it. I found myself checking the date over and over, because it seemed impossible to me that the APA would publish a credulous article about the IAT in the Year of Our Lord 2025. Alas, that's what they did.

A bit of background: The IAT is a reaction-time test anyone can take on their computer or phone which ostensibly reveals the test-taker's level of implicit (unconscious) bias toward and against various groups. The most famous version in the United States is the black-white IAT, which reveals whether a person favors white people, black people, or is one of those saintly few who exhibit little or no implicit bias at all. (The results are normalized to a scale ranging from -1 to 1, with 0 indicating the absence of bias in either direction.)

The implicit association test was formally introduced to the public in 1998 during a press conference in Seattle held by its co-founders, the psychology professors Anthony Greenwald (University of Washington) and Mahzarin Banaji (Harvard University). The headline of the accompanying UW press release made it sound like Greenwald and Banaji had exposed a veritable epidemic: "Roots of unconscious prejudice affect 90 to 95 percent of people, psychologists demonstrate at press conference."[2]

This test soon went mega-viral, becoming a mainstay of diversity trainings and, perhaps more importantly, our national conversation about race and racism (it was certainly helped along by Project Implicit, a Harvard-affiliated website where anyone could take various IATs). At the risk of invoking for the umpteenth time the strained metaphor involving quantum mechanics, the very act of measuring something has an impact on the thing being measured. As soon as Greenwald and Banaji provided the world with (what appeared to be) cold, hard data supporting certain claims about America's intractable race problems, implicit bias became *the* favored way to talk about those problems, at least in many elite circles.

I should admit to being a bit of an IAT obsessive. I wrote an in-depth article critiquing the test for the website of *New York Magazine* in 2017,[3] when I was on staff there, which I believe was the first such longform treatment of the IAT and its applications. I then adapted and updated that article and published it as a chapter in my 2021 book *The Quick Fix: Why Fad Psychology Can't Cure Our Social Ills*.[4]

A full accounting of the problems with the IAT and how it has been interpreted by countless academic journal articles and mass-media treatments is well beyond the scope of this chapter. But, in brief:

- It's true that the IAT has generated some reliable and replicable patterns of results. For example, white Americans are indeed quicker to link images of Black people to negative terms than to positive ones, on average. But it has never been established, to any degree of certainty, that these patterns represent accurate measures of implicit bias, *per se*. There were always other potential explanations for the patterns of results the researchers observed, ranging from reaction time to familiarity *with* stereotypes (as opposed to an endorsement *of* them) to political orientation, with significant amounts of random noise, as well as measurement error. In one brilliant 2006 experiment, a team of researchers introduced study participants to two nonexistent groups, the Noffians and the Fasites. Then, after various experimental manipulations, the subjects took IAT tests measuring their implicit bias toward/against Noffians and Fasites. As the authors wrote, "participants were faster to associate Noffians with 'Bad' after being conditioned to associate Noffians with oppression, victimization, and discrimination."[5] In other words, telling subjects that the Noffians were oppressed elicited an IAT response that the test interpreted as bias *against* that group.
- It was never established, with any degree of certainty, how large a role implicit bias plays in observed racial discrepancies, versus countless other potential explanations for those discrepancies. And yet the architects of the IAT, as well as the academics and journalists who treated it favorably, have prematurely accepted the assumption that implicit bias is a big part of the story. For example, Banaji

and Greenwald argued in their 2013 book *Blindspot* that "it is reasonable to conclude not only that implicit bias is a cause of Black disadvantage but also that it plausibly plays a greater role than does explicit bias in explaining the discrimination that contributes to Black disadvantage."[6] But whether and to what extent we even need implicit bias to explain lingering racial discrepancies in the US is itself an open and unanswered question, given the existence of other, more parsimonious explanations.

- While the researchers produced many studies claiming a link between IAT tests and real-world behavior, this link was tenuous at best. In an important 2019 meta-analysis, a team led by Patrick Forscher and including Brian Nosek—one of the original proponents of the test—found that differences in IAT scores accounted for about 1 percent of the variance in behavior observed in lab-based IAT experiments.[7] That same meta-analysis found no evidence of effective interventions to reduce implicit bias or biased behavior (supposedly) caused by it.

The IAT raced out of the gate and gained tremendous momentum before it had been fully validated, generating a frenzy of academic activity and rerouting the American conversation about race and racism. Well after the critics had their say[8] and the aforementioned questions were well-disseminated, still it shuffled along as a zombie idea, continuing to exert influence. The most important professional association for research psychologists in the country was *still* comfortable presenting it as valid and proven in 2025. "The IAT has not been without its detractors, some of whom have argued that associations between IAT scores and real-world discrimination or biased behavior are weak," explains the APA blog post. "Yet various meta-analyses have repeatedly found support for the test's validity." This is inaccurate.

Unfortunately, this chain of events isn't unusual, and there are plenty of other examples.[9] Explaining why this happens is, again, beyond the purview of this chapter. Instead, I want to make a speculative case that viewpoint diversity within academia could serve as a rather reliable inoculation against these occurrences.

This is a theoretical argument, but I'd argue it's a well-grounded one. We already know that diversity of any sort brings both potential upsides and downsides. One feature of diversity that is often presented as a downside is friction: If an established community has a certain set of agreed-upon social, religious, or other norms or beliefs, and a new group settles in the area with their *own* norms or beliefs, naturally this causes friction. It can be a productive friction that eventually generates interesting new cultural innovations and amalgamations, but it is friction nonetheless, and in the worst cases it can cause bloodshed. *We worshipped these gods until this other tribe moved in next door, worshipping other gods*. What once was smooth is smooth no longer.

But academic research *shouldn't* be smooth; if viewpoint diversity indeed brings friction to academic processes, that might be a good thing. Simply put, if you have a group of people who are all on the same page, whether ideologically, religiously, or academically, certain untested assumptions can sneak into the progress, causing everyone involved to get a bit over their skis. Contrariwise, in groups where there *is* viewpoint diversity, that likely makes it easier for dissenters to notice flaws in an argument or a research agenda, to point them out, and to convince the group to hit the brakes when doing so is warranted.

While viewpoint diversity isn't *just* about political ideology, political ideology is part of the story here. The IAT is the brainchild of social psychologists, and the data we have suggests that social psychology is a particularly liberal area, even by the standards of research psychology. When the social psychologists Yoel Inbar and Joris Lammers surveyed a sample of social and personality psychologists,[10] for example, their results were jarring: Just 6 percent of respondents said they identified as conservative.[11]

No research project springs from thin air; they are all undergirded by certain preexisting beliefs about what deserves funding, which questions need answering, and which assumptions can be, well, assumed. The Implicit Association Test is no exception: This project was founded because the researchers believed that ongoing racial discrimination is a major policy concern; that a significant proportion of this discrimination occurs unconsciously; that they had found a reasonably rigorous way to measure this form of discrimination; and (later) that it was responsible to allow the public to take this test at home, potentially eliciting a negative psychological response. These are generally left-of-center coded beliefs, meaning the implicit bias research project itself came into the world driven, in part, by bias.

But going beyond partisan politics, we can note other assumptions: For instance, the IAT's enthusiasts all agreed that it made sense to fight racism and racial disparities by measuring and intervening on individual actors, potentially on a mass scale. This is such a natural thing for social psychologists to do that they might not even recognize it *as* an assumption, but that's exactly what it is. It isn't necessarily the case that individual measurement and tweaks can meaningfully address something as complicated as racial discrepancies, but everyone in the IAT camp agreed on this front. This also highlights the limitations of making this about left-versus-right; from a left-wing perspective, the IAT could be accused of not taking a "structural" enough approach to attacking racial disparities, settling for nudge-y "neoliberal" interventions instead.

So, imagine a world in which, early on in the development of a research program like the IAT, its assumptions were subjected to evaluation by some sort of panel of qualified experts specifically chosen for their viewpoint diversity. To be clear, I know that this is a far-fetched fantasy—I might as well have this hypothetical panel consist of unicorns—but bear with me.

If the early beliefs fueling the IAT faced real scrutiny from those who did *not* share Banaji and Greenwald's priors, it might have saved us all some time—not to mention a great deal of money and effort—in the long run. It turned out that, being human beings, Banaji and Greenwald were strongly convinced of claims that turned out to be unproven. And their colleagues, cut as they were from the same ideological cloth, likely shared those beliefs (or viewpoints, if you like). Even if they disagreed on some of the specifics, it's *hard* to express disagreement about political beliefs held sacred by your own tribe to your fellow tribespeople. Doing so can risk a very visceral feeling of judgment or, in the worst cases, real social or professional consequences. It's not for nothing that when I first contacted Banaji about this controversy for my *New York* article, she responded, "The IAT scares people who say things like 'look, the water fountains are desegregated, what's your problem?'"

Being accused of harboring base motives is far less of a concern in an ideologically diverse group, because it's *assumed* there will be disagreement. If I, a liberal, were sitting at a table with a bunch of Trump supporters, there'd be no meaningful cost to expressing my skepticism of Trump, because the conversation would be occurring across political lines. Discussions consisting solely of members of the same group entail a far greater risk of self-censorship and, if disagreement emerges at all, of undue sanction.

I obviously can't *prove* this would make a difference in a case like the IAT's premature rollout and celebration. This isn't the sort of thing you can submit to a randomized controlled trial. What I can say, as a journalist who has covered many controversies at the intersection of science and public policy for almost a decade and a half, is that the prevailing ideologies of scientists (and the journalists who cover their work) certainly *seem* to matter a great deal. Why wouldn't they? What possible case is there to make that ideological conformity *doesn't* unduly lubricate the path from the conception of an idea to its publication and real-world application? Does anyone actually think that the IAT would have been disseminated as quickly if it had been born in a milieu of genuine viewpoint diversity?

I need to be careful here, because I am speculating in the absence of data. It's also important to note that ideas get adopted prematurely not *just* because of ideological conformity, but also for other, more basic reasons: If you're a young scholar in any field, you're going to feel a gravitational pull toward whatever the currently dominant paradigms are. When implicit bias was the dominant paradigm in discrimination research, young social psychologists were incentivized to study it and—if they were lucky—to produce a paper or two that incrementally advanced our understanding of the subject without criticizing it too harshly. That's how you advance in a field: Skeptics tend to have a bad time, particularly young ones who lack the influence and job security to meaningfully criticize incumbent ideas.

But it seems silly, at this juncture, to deny the downsides of viewpoint homogeneity, especially given how poorly the social sciences have fared in recent years, with their multiple replication crises. I know that some researchers have argued that political bias cannot explain these problems,[12] but whether or not that's the case, what conceivable downside could there be to introducing more political diversity to the process, some way or another? Could it possibly make things any worse?

I wish I could conclude this chapter with exciting, concrete solutions. Alas, my ideas are pretty well-aged at this point: It isn't healthy that only 6 percent of psychologists (or any other type of researcher) identifies as conservative. That suggests something is seriously amiss, and whether the bias against conservatives is implicit or explicit—or whether conservatives are underrepresented for other reasons altogether—until this problem is addressed and more viewpoint diversity is introduced into the field, social psychology will be missing some much-needed friction.

Notes

1 Kirsten Weir, "The implicit association test: Shining a light on hidden beliefs," American Psychological Association, May 14, 2025, https://www.apa.org/research-practice/conduct-research/hidden-association.

2 Joel Schwarz, "Roots of unconscious prejudice affect 90 to 95 percent of people, psychologists demonstrate at press conference," University of Washington, September 29, 1998, https://www.washington.edu/news/1998/09/29/roots-of-unconscious-prejudice-affect-90-to-95-percent-of-people-psychologists-demonstrate-at-press-conference.

3 Jesse Singal, "Psychology's Favorite Tool for Measuring Racism Isn't Up to the Job," *New York Magazine*, https://www.thecut.com/2017/01/psychologys-racism-measuring-tool-isnt-up-to-the-job.html.

4 Jesse Singal, *The Quick Fix* (Farrar, Straus and Giroux, 2021), https://www.amazon.com/Quick-Fix-Psychology-Cant-Social/dp/0374239800.

5 Eric Luis Uhlmann, Victoria L. Brescoll, and Elizabeth Levy Paluck, "Are members of low status groups perceived as bad, or badly off? Egalitarian negative associations and automatic prejudice," *Journal of Experimental Social Psychology* 42 (2006): 491–99, https://www.socialjudgments.com/docs/Uhlmann%20Brescoll%20and%20Paluck%202006.pdf.

6 Mahzarin R. Banahi and Anthony G. Greenwald, *Blind Spot: Hidden Biases of Good People* (Delacorte Press, 2013).

7 Patrick S. Forscher, et al., "A meta-analysis of procedures to change implicit measures," Journal of Personality and Social Psychology 117, no. 3 (2019): 522–559, https://psycnet.apa.org/record/2019-31306-001.

8 As early as 2004, the star psychologist Phil Tetlock had published a critical article about the test which he coauthored with Hal Arkes. Other critiques soon followed, with scholars like Hart Blanton, Gregory Mitchell, Fred Oswald, and James Jaccard making key contributions. If any of this work had an impact on academic and public public enthusiasm for the IAT in the aughts and early 2010s, it appears to have been minor at best.

9 Drawing only on subjects that I myself have written about and which generated real-world interventions, I'd argue that this general storyline applies to microaggressions research, power posing, the (ostensibly) anti-PTSD military program Comprehensive Soldier Fitness, the concept of "grit" as an explanatory factor in educational inequality, and an extremely high percentage of diversity trainings. Suffice it to say that this is a very limited sampling.

10 Yoel Inbar and Joris Lammers, "Political Diversity in Social and Personality Psychology," *Perspectives on Psychological Science* 7, no. 5 (2012): 1–8, https://yoelinbar.net/papers/political_diversity.pdf.

11 It's important to note that Inbar and Lammers argue that, when they break this question out into specific areas, the results aren't quite so lopsided, with decently sized subsets of the sample describing themselves as "moderate" on "foreign policy" and "the economy." Still, nothing in their paper runs contrary to the idea that overall, social and personality psychology are dominated by researchers who sit firmly on the Left.

12 See here for a study finding no direct correlation between researchers' political slant and replicability of their studies: https://journals.sagepub.com/doi/full/10.1177/1745691620924463.

Pluralism on Campus: Should Colleges De-Register Student Groups? Exploring Campus Pluralism Through the Lens of the University of Iowa's All-Comers Controversy

by Eboo Patel with Rollie Olson

College campuses are one of the few places in American life that offer a daily opportunity for cooperation across difference. From biology labs to intramural badminton courts, people of diverse identities and divergent ideologies come together in shared spaces and work on shared projects. At their best, campuses model not only demographic diversity but also viewpoint diversity, giving students a chance to encounter, and work alongside, people who think differently about the world.

But these ripe opportunities for pluralism on campus don't mean the absence of conflict. On the contrary, campuses are *designed* to be laboratories of difference, as places where disagreement is expected, especially around questions of identity and belief. In a Tocquevillian sense, students forming associations

This essay reflects Eboo Patel's perspective and personal experiences. Rollie Olson contributed as co-author and editor, helping shape and refine the narrative.

around deeply held convictions is a democratic good. Yet the organization of student groups around particular identities and beliefs, while often a strength of campus life, can also pose some of the most difficult dilemmas—and revealing opportunities—for college administrators seeking to positively engage diversity. The University of Iowa's 2017 all-comers controversy shows just how complex and consequential those tensions can be.

The Iowa All-Comers Controversy and the Cost of Consistency

A University of Iowa student group with about ten members called Business Leaders in Christ (BLinC) did not allow an openly gay student to fill a leadership position at the organization, claiming that LGBT identity/sexual activity was in violation of the group's statement of faith. As a result, administrators at the University of Iowa deregistered the student group, citing the University's human rights policy, which says student groups should be open to anyone regardless of race, color, creed, religion, or other identity, with special attention to protected classes.

BLinC pointed out that *lots of student groups* are based around particular identities and affinities, and such associations generally reserve certain privileges for people who share those identities and affinities, thereby excluding people who do not. If the University was going to deregister BLinC, what was it going to do about the Imam Mahdi group, which wants its leaders to be Shia Muslim students? Or the Korean American Student Association? Students For Life? The Feminist Union? Would they all be required to have governing documents that complied with the University of Iowa's human rights policy?

It turns out that, out of 513 student organizations at the University of Iowa, just 157 were in compliance with the University's human rights policy. *That means a whopping 356 were out of line.*

A federal judge, in ordering that BLinC be temporarily

reinstated as an official student organization, wondered why the University had applied its policy so unevenly. That temporary reinstatement became permanent. In 2019, a federal court ruled that the University of Iowa had unconstitutionally discriminated against BLinC. The court ordered the group reinstated. Initially, administrators were granted qualified immunity, but in 2021, the Eighth Circuit ruled they could be held personally liable for violating BLinC's constitutional rights.

Looking back, I find this case extremely important and not at all easy.

It's important because one of the distinctive qualities of the United States is its thriving civil society, that area of public life that is generally apart from commercial interests and is not principally dictated by the state. A civil society is formed by people who create voluntary associations, often around a particular identity. In some parts of the world, such civic groups can be identity-based militias engulfed in an internal civil war. In the United States, more often than not, diverse civic groups both express their particular identities and cooperate positively with others.

Campuses are one of the places where young people learn how to do this. When the College Democrats and the College Republicans organize a political debate on campus, they are both expressing their distinctive identities and contributing to the campus's viewpoint diversity, strengthening a public square that makes space for divergent convictions. The latter depends on the former. In other words, cooperation between identity groups can only take place if there are identity groups to begin with.

What makes this case difficult? Put simply: There are multiple competing values at play. One is the value around protecting people from harm, especially historically marginalized groups. Can you imagine being the gay student who was told he couldn't run for the leadership role in that student organization? It tightens my throat to even think about it. Good for the administrators at the University of Iowa for wanting to protect that student's dignity.

But what happens when applying that human rights policy violates another value: the principle of identity-based groups being allowed to define their own identities? Defining identity means, at some level, excluding others. The University of Iowa, for example, boasts about being a premier public research university. It excludes (discriminates against) applicants whose grades and test scores do not meet its definition of "premier."

This case sits at the intersection of competing values: protecting historically marginalized students from harm, sustaining viewpoint diversity by allowing identity-based groups to define themselves, and deciding when and how institutions should use coercive power. It also raises deeper questions about what we mean by diversity and pluralism, the distinctive role religion plays in identity formation, and how power shapes which groups' administrators instinctively support and which they view with suspicion.

Throughout this essay, I'll draw on John Inazu's *Confident Pluralism* for its clear legal framing and thoughtful take on what it means to build a healthy, diverse democracy.

Here's a thought exercise: Imagine a scenario where the person/group at the center would evoke some instinctive sympathy. Here is such a case:

Let's say that the acronym BLinC does not stand for Business Leaders in Christ (the student group at the center of the initial storm at Iowa), but rather Black Leaders in Christ. It's a group for African American Christians and it has a distinguished record of providing emotional and spiritual support for a racial minority on campus in a way that helps its members thrive, in the classroom and beyond. In fact, let's say a university study showed that Black students involved in Black Leaders in Christ graduated at a significantly higher rate than other Black students. In interviews, those graduates pointed to their involvement in BLinC as a key reason for this.

There are all kinds of students who attend the meetings, social events, worship services, and volunteer projects of Black Leaders in Christ. There are white kids, Korean Americans, Indian

Americans, etc. But the leadership of the group is reserved for African American Christians.

A Puerto Rican student decides to run for president. She is gently told that there are plenty of other places for her to offer leadership, but she cannot run for the exec board. If you are a university administrator, do you ask Black Leaders in Christ to change its policy and practice or else be de-registered?

Now let's say the group is called BMinC—Black *Men* in Christ. The mission statement of the group underscores the particular challenges Black men face in American society. The purpose of BMinC is to provide special spiritual, social, and emotional support for that particular group. In this case, all activities are reserved for Black men. Let's say the difference in graduation rates for participants in this group versus other Black men on campus is even more stark.

Do you begin de-registration proceedings?

What if Black Men in Christ has the same kind of policies around sexual identity/expression that many other conservative religious groups have (this would include not just Christians but many Muslims, Jews, and Hindus as well), and effectively bars openly gay students from running for office. Does that trigger de-registration?

As you can see, these questions get thorny fast.

Religious Identity on Campus

I belong to a religious community that excludes my wife. I'm an Ismaili Muslim; she's Sunni. In our tradition, only those who profess formal belief in the Imam, the community's spiritual leader and interpreter of the faith, may enter certain religious spaces or participate in core rituals. That means when I take our children to prayer, my wife cannot come with us. It's painful for both of us.

These rules aren't up for debate. Ismaili leadership is inherited, not elected, and the boundaries of belief are drawn from within the tradition itself. While the specifics of the faith may be unique, the pattern isn't. Many religious communities have boundaries that include some and exclude others. Non-Muslims cannot enter Mecca, non-Catholics cannot receive communion, and only men can become priests in the Catholic and LDS churches.

Generally, there are not enough Ismailis at a college to form an official Ismaili Students Association. If there were, it would surely say that at least the leaders of the group needed to be Ismaili. How could the leaders of a religiously-oriented group be *unable* to enter the prayer hall of that group?

Under all-comers policies, a college would have to de-register an Ismaili Students Association. That would obviously negatively impact Ismaili students, who would lose access to college facilities and also lose the ability to advertise widely. It would also negatively impact the wider campus community. Ismailis love running social events and organizing service projects or awareness campaigns about humanitarian issues in Central and South Asia—all are open to everyone. The group would also be part of the diverse civil society of the campus, and by their presence educate people about the range of religious and cultural groups on the planet.

Doesn't a college campus have a stake in the flourishing of identity groups like a hypothetical Ismaili Students Association? Doesn't a diverse civic fabric require strong individual threads, including religious ones?

One important criticism of all-comers policies is that they ignore how religious identities function. As my friend Greg Jao of InterVarsity Christian Fellowship has said, members of religious communities do not generally get to vote on their doctrines on a regular basis. The belief is understood to have been established not in the material world of democratic citizenship, but in a cosmic world where different authorities reign.

What further complicates this is that different religious communities operate in remarkably varied ways. For example, Ismailis have a highly centralized authority structure while Unitarians are highly decentralized and typically do their own thing from church to church and group to group.

Student affairs may be unfamiliar with how Ismailis function, and it would be a sad situation if the first time a college administrator substantively interacted with the Ismaili group was to force it into compliance on an all-comers policy rather than to appreciate the group's contribution to campus. One of my central criticisms about all-comers policies is how they frame religious groups as a problem to be solved rather than as gift to be celebrated.

An Ismaili group gently telling a non-Ismaili she can't run for office rarely raises concern. But when an Evangelical group bars a gay student from leadership, it sets off a five-alarm fire—despite the fact that groups like InterVarsity also exclude leaders for doctrinal reasons, such as premarital heterosexual sex or rejecting the Trinity, and yet rarely face administrative action.

I find anti-gay exclusion offensive and hurtful. When a gay student is excluded because of his/her/their identity or expression, I instinctively want to help that individual. I can see myself reaching into my toolkit as an administrator and doing whatever I can to help that gay student and to send a message.

But a whole set of problems emerges when the instinct to protect a gay student from being excluded by a Christian group is turned into a general all-comers policy.

As soon as you click one level up in principle/policy/abstraction from the instinct, you catch a whole bunch of other groups in your net. You kick off the Feminist Union, the Pro-Life group, the Ismaili Students Association. You may even find yourself pressuring the LGBT group to change its charter.

A further example: Most Muslim groups have a practice of men leading prayers and giving religious sermons (Ismailis are an exception to this). I am not aware of this practice causing their de-registering or the triggering of a general-application all-comers policy, although it is certain to come under scrutiny once such a policy is announced.

So, what is it about Evangelical groups and the particular exclusion of gay students that sets off alarm bells in the minds of college administrators?

Confident Pluralism: Rethinking Administrative Power

Among college administrators, there is an instinctive sympathy for gay students and the marginalization many have experienced, an instinct I find highly commendable.

In my experience over years of visiting campuses across the country, there is also an instinctive suspicion of Evangelical Christianity, which many administrators associate principally with the marginalization of gay students and women—often shaped by their negative personal experiences with conservative churches.

Despite how these personal encounters in one's hometown church shape one's perception of a religious community, to harbor ill will towards Christian student groups because of this is unprofessional. Consider if a secular Muslim or culturally Hindu administrator cited anti-gay discrimination or sexism at a hometown mosque or temple (it's not like such things never happen) for their derogatory treatment of the campus Muslim or Hindu group.

This leaves the best reason for the instinctive suspicion that many college administrators harbor toward Evangelical Christian groups: their power.

The logic goes like this. Conservative Christians are in the halls of power in Washington with both the penchant for and the ability to legislate discrimination against groups they do not like, including gay people.

What does this have to do with Evangelical student groups on campus? I predict that administrators are too closely associating the first-year student from rural Tennessee playing guitar at the InterVarsity Bible study and Franklin Graham as part of one big movement seeking to legislate conservative Christianity. From that vantage point, it's understandable that some administrators would view these small student groups with heightened concern, as if denying them a foothold is necessary to protect the values they see under threat.

The fact, however, is that many of these Evangelical student groups are very small, making this a tortured logic. Business Leaders in Christ at the University of Iowa reportedly had about ten students. A similar group that Bowdoin College de-registered had about twenty-five active members.

Most importantly, none of these groups are trying to legislate conservative Christianity on campus. They're small, often countercultural, and focused on living out their values. In many cases, they share space with people they deeply disagree with, all under the shared understanding that everyone has the right to express and associate as they wish. That freedom is guaranteed by American law and is the genius of our civil society. Indeed, religious groups enjoy additional protections under the Constitution, through legislation like the Religious Freedom Restoration Act, and in Supreme Court decisions like *Hosanna-Tabor*, which affirmed the right of faith communities to choose their own leaders. At the same time, the Court has drawn boundaries. In *Christian Legal Society v. Martinez* (2010), it upheld a university's decision to deny recognition to a student group that required leaders to affirm a heterosexual-only sexual ethic. Clearly, these situations are challenging.

One especially important consequence of the debate around all-comers policies is that Evangelical Christian groups, in coalition with a diverse group of those with whom they theologically disagree, are advocating for freedom of association for *everyone*, rather than making a case for Christian conservatism to reign supreme. This is an illustration of our democracy's strength, and I believe, of genuine good will.

College administrators ought to be taking their cues from these interesting civic collaborations. As John Inazu writes in *Confident Pluralism*, administrative authorities (especially the government) ought to be protecting people's differences—their rights to express, associate, and assemble as they wish—especially when they go against majoritarian norms. He writes, "We cannot begin with the premise that the public forum is open to all groups and then start excluding those groups we don't like."

At the very least, administrative authorities ought to exercise extreme caution when using coercive power against student groups. Not only are good general policies nearly impossible to come by, the concentration of power should put fear in the hearts of anyone who cares about liberal democracy. Once that sword is brought out against this group on that issue, it can too easily be brought ought again and again.

There are limits to this, of course. No university should allow a KKK group or a pro-pedophile group to stand. And there are very difficult cases, for example the *Bob Jones* decision where the Supreme Court found that it was constitutionally legal for the federal government to revoke the tax-exempt status of a private Christian college for its racist policy barring interracial dating. I agree with that decision, even though it was the federal government using coercive power against a private association, because I think the particular circumstances of 400 years of institutionalized racism demanded an exception to the general rule of identity-associations being allowed to constitute themselves.

Are gay rights analogous to issues of racial equality? Although the system of slavery and segregation in the United States is *sui generis*, I think an argument can be made that there needs to be similar government/administrator intervention to root out homophobia and heterosexism.

I am instinctively sympathetic to this, but I worry that more harm than good is done in the process, especially because it grants administrative authorities too much power and uses a specific case to drive general policies with a host of negative effects, like requiring you to de-register student groups that you actually want to support.

We should instead define a diverse civil society as a place where people with different identities and deep disagreements can collectively flourish by respecting one another's identities, building relationships across disagreements, and cooperating where they can to serve the common good. The First Amendment of our Constitution with its protections of expression, association, and assembly provides for this. The great Jesuit political philosopher John Courtney Murray called these provisions our "articles of peace." In a similar vein, Inazu writes, "The protections of assembly are part of our mutual nonaggression pact. They extend to groups that we like and groups that we don't like."

So how can college administrators who seek (as they should) to be supportive of gay students do more good than harm? Here's my suggestion: *Use your programmatic powers instead of your coercive ones.* Help those students start religious groups that are gay friendly (virtually every liberal protestant denomination in the United States has a wing that is LGBT-affirming). Send them to conferences. Spend time talking to them. Find them mentors. Make it clear that you want them to thrive but your basket has lots of carrots and very few sticks.

Interestingly, there are a number of gay individuals and groups who prefer it this way. In other words, who *do not want* administrative authorities to use coercive power to vanquish groups that they don't like, even ones that exclude them.

This position makes perfect sense when you consider that, not so long ago, administrators tried to use their coercive powers to *ban LGBT groups*. In the early 1970s, the University of New Hampshire tried to shut down a gay student group. In 1974, a federal court ruled against the administrative authorities at the University, siding with the gay student group and affirming its rights to expression, assembly, and association. Interestingly, such groups, according to law professor Dale Carpenter (quoted in Inazu's book), "historically discriminated in membership based on sexual orientation . . . even groups that are not exclusively gay would resist having heterosexuals in leadership position."

In other words, to maintain their understanding of their identity-association, they excluded others. This shouldn't surprise anyone it's simply the way identity and affinity groups function.

It also raises this uncomfortable possibility: An administrator who, on one day, applies an all-comers policy to force an Evangelical group to include a gay student in leadership might the next day find herself, because of that same policy, forcing the LGBT group to accept leaders it believes are inconsistent with its mission.

As Inazu notes in his book, the phrase *confident pluralism* actually comes from a gay rights group that came out *against* all-comers policies. They might not have liked the religious groups that excluded people in their community, but they preferred to engage them in dialogue in the public square rather than have administrative authorities use coercive powers. Gays and Lesbians for Individual Liberty (whose mission is the "tolerance and acceptance of homosexuals among members of the wider society") filed a legal brief which stated: "the First Amendment envisions a . . . *confident pluralism* that conduces to civil peace and advances democratic consensus-building."

Supporters of all-comers policies could argue that requiring every student group to be open to all students is more inclusive of divergent perspectives, therefore maximizing viewpoint diversity. In practice, by forcing groups to flatten the boundaries of their particularities, we undermine the very differences that make diversity meaningful. After all, diversity is not just the differences we like. An alternative view—one I believe is more consistent with the pluralist tradition—is that viewpoint diversity is best supported when a wide range of groups, including those formed around strong shared beliefs, are free to constitute themselves on their own terms. In this view, the university empowers a diverse ecosystem of student associations—some more welcoming, some exclusive, all contributing in different ways to a richer campus life.

As a great laboratory of American democracy, the most essential work of a college campus is to sustain civil disagreement, where convictions are reasoned through, voiced with integrity, and woven into the fabric of campus life.

Viewpoint Diversity—Up to a Point

by Bret Stephens

(Originally published in *SAPIR*, March 3, 2025)

Not long ago I was invited to share a stage with a well-known Jewish writer whose political views had, over the years, shifted from center-left Zionism to far-left anti-Zionism. The two of us had previously appeared in at least a dozen public events and, notwithstanding our deep political differences, had an amicable offstage relationship. There was also a generous honorarium on offer.

This time, however, something in me revolted at the thought of seeing my name next to his. I told the organizer that I would not share a platform with him. Not after October 7. Not for any amount of money. Never again.

That was a gut call. Was it the right one? I have spent years making the case—in newspaper columns, commencement speeches, and essays in *SAPIR*—not just for free speech but also for the importance of dialogue and debate, of listening and keeping an open mind, of encouraging a multiplicity of views and engaging those with whom we profoundly disagree.

"Befriend your intellectual adversaries," I urged one graduating class of college seniors in 2017. "Assume that they're smart, that their motives are honorable, and that they are your fellow travelers in a quest to better understand a common set of challenges. Master the civilized art of agreeable disagreement. . . . Have an argument, then have a drink together."

Do I still believe that? Yes, but...

The term *viewpoint diversity* has been gaining traction in recent years, particularly in academia. Since *SAPIR*'s previous issue on "The University," I've been thinking about the relationship between the two.

It's easy to see why universities have become the main battle grounds for advancing viewpoint diversity. College and university presidents recognize (or have been made to recognize by angry alumni and alarmed trustees) that many of their schools have become left-wing ideological monocultures. These presidents understand—in theory, at least—that the contestation of ideas is critical to pedagogical and knowledge-seeking enterprises. And they already have a diversity rubric into which they can easily slot the word *viewpoint*, thereby adding it to the list of other diversities they claim to treasure: racial, ethnic, sexual, gender, and so on.

All this is a good start, at least when it's treated as something more than window dressing. Ideological echo chambers are almost always intellectually deadening. Differing views on fundamental questions can help stimulate important conversations, challenge unexamined assumptions, sharpen both sides of a debate, and remind people that the truth is rarely simple and that nobody has exclusive claims to it. And if communities and institutions are supposed to be enriched by including people of diverse identities, why not extend the principle to include those with diverse opinions?

Still, there are some shortcomings with this version of "diversity." Three come to mind:

- First, promoting multiple views within a community hardly guarantees that they'll come into the sort of fruitful contact that can generate intellectual excitement and new ideas. Other plausible outcomes of viewpoint diversity include provoking conflict or mutual avoidance between antagonistic groups, or the tokenized representation of certain (usually conservative) views.

- Second, the ultimate purpose of intellectual inquiry isn't diversity. It's truth. Declaring an interest in "viewpoint diversity," especially in academic settings, risks mistaking a means for an end.
- Third, virtually every institution—including those with a sincere commitment to free speech—will have defensible reasons not to tolerate certain extreme or damaging views: Where does one draw the line when the principle of diversity itself has no limits? At its worst, viewpoint diversity can become an easy way for institutions to dodge important, if difficult, moral questions.

I had a taste of the first shortcoming a few weeks after October 7, when, at the behest of a concerned alumnus, I was invited to offer a pro-Israel perspective at an elite New England college. I arrived on campus to learn that, at the hour I was scheduled to speak in one auditorium, a pro-Palestinian counter-event had been organized in a separate venue. Both events proceeded without incident, and the college could now claim that it had fostered viewpoint diversity. Holding the events simultaneously also lessened the chances of heckling, protest, or something else untoward.

But what the school had mainly done was undermine the strongest rationale for the two events: namely, to expose students to views of the conflict that might be different from their own. Instead of creating spaces for robust engagement and challenge, what the college achieved was a convenient form of viewpoint ghettoization.

This is a problem that confronts universities broadly, particularly those that are struggling to bring more ideologically diverse (read: nonprogressive) thinkers to campus as speakers, students, faculty, and administrators. It's always possible to set up an island of political dissent on liberal campuses: Yale has the Buckley

Institute, Stanford has the Hoover Institution, law schools have their Federalist Societies, and Princeton has Robert George. Yet all this exists at a remove from the host institutions. Independent or right-of-center thinkers rarely have much of a hand in shaping academic programs, admissions policies, tenure decisions, or any of the other core functions through which left-wing faculty and staff have shaped left-wing institutions.

Could universities do better? Yes, but it would take much more than just inviting a few conservative speakers, hiring some independent-minded scholars, or admitting students with non-progressive inclinations. Above all, it requires a paradigm shift, one that the term *diversity*—in both its original sense and in its links to DEI—is ill-suited to accommodate. That shift begins with the recognition that viewpoint diversity, in an academic setting, must mean more than coexistence among different opinions or the presence of a few tokenized contrarian voices. It asks for curiosity, conversation, challenge, contestation—in a word, engagement. It means a set of mental habits and institutional practices that goes beyond the current buffet-table vision of viewpoint diversity. And it depends on academic leaders who believe that the core task of the university is to promote a culture of civil disagreement, however much resistance that generates on campus. Accomplishing this is the work of decades.

Universities need something else: a rededication to the pursuit of *veritas*.

Truth, at least outside of a few scientific disciplines, is a difficult idea because it's almost always contested. We also know from experience that individuals, institutions, and governments that make absolute claims to the truth tend, when given the opportunity, to exercise those claims both despotically and dishonestly. In democracies, our response to that risk is pluralism and tolerance—allowing different conceptions of the truth to coexist at a safe and happy distance, or to interact only voluntarily.

But even democracies still require truth. And universities aren't democracies.

Indeed, among the roles a university ought to play in a democracy is to act as a *counterweight* to the viewpoint diversity that already exists in society—that is, to provide authoritative sources of information about what *is* true amid a country's diverse (and sometimes dangerous) views about the truth. To take a whimsical example: If Congress were to pass, and the president were to sign, legislation declaring that candy is good for you, or that slavery was a benevolent institution, it would be the essential role of university experts to say: No, it isn't, and no, it wasn't. Or take a real-world example: When a fraudulent private historian, David Irving, insisted the Holocaust never happened, it took a real academic historian, Emory's Deborah Lipstadt, to demonstrate to a British court that it had.

At their best, universities have been able to play this role because the expertise they offer is well-earned, well-vetted, and well-measured—and therefore widely trusted. Yet, too many universities have been failing at this role for years, which is one reason public trust in them has collapsed. The reasons for that failure are many and go beyond the scope of this essay. But part of the explanation is that the place of viewpoint diversity on campuses has undergone a kind of inversion. Whereas universities used to solicit diverse views as a means of pursuing truth, now those same universities suppress diverse views while insisting that there is no ultimate truth, merely different "narratives," "lived experiences," or "commitments."

To mend themselves, universities will need to regain two forms of confidence: the confidence to insist that truth is, in most cases, objective and ascertainable, and that it deserves to be defended against the emotions, opinions, or preferences of those who deny it; and next, the confidence to invite careful examination of a broad variety of opinions and hypotheses about what the truth might be.

This brings me to viewpoint diversity's third shortcoming.

In his 1983 book, *Statecraft as Soulcraft*, the columnist George

Will wrote, "The most important four words in politics are 'up to a point.'" He elaborated: "Are we in favor of free speech? Of course—up to a point. Are we for liberty, equality, military strength, industrial vigor, environmental protection, traffic safety? Up to a point."

The same might be said about viewpoint diversity. Should today's universities have much more of it? Of course, up to a point. There's a lot to be said for bringing more independent thinkers to campus—people who never sit comfortably in any sort of ideological box, who like arguing with their peers, who treat skepticism as a virtue, who delight in discussing or delivering a provocative idea. But there's a line between an iconoclast and a crank, a skeptic and a cynic, a gadfly and a hater. That line isn't always easily drawn. But it's the responsibility of university presidents, provosts, deans, and department heads to find and enforce it.

Much of the problem with the practice of viewpoint diversity is that faculty and administrators set tight lines when it comes to one side of the political spectrum but not the other. That's how it was possible for MIT to host Dalia Mogahed, a scholar of Muslim studies and proud defender of the October 7 pogrom, while refusing to host a talk by Middle East negotiator Dennis Ross. (The university relented after the rejection became a public embarrassment.) That's also how a trans activist like Alejandra Caraballo is invited to teach at Harvard, despite a record of inciteful ad hominem attacks,[1] while the respected evolutionary biologist Carole Hooven is hounded off the campus[2] because she insists sex differences are real.

These double standards are a serious problem—but they are not the whole problem.

Universities, even those that profess a commitment to free expression and seek to live up to it, are, in fact, entitled to set certain limits about the views (and students) they do or don't admit. They may aim to set wide boundaries on *what* can or cannot be said freely, but they also set narrow boundaries on *who* may or may not speak freely. They do this through rigorous admissions, hiring, promotion, and retention practices: that is, by choosing who gets to belong to a community dedicated to the pursuit of truth. That pursuit requires a combination of virtues: intellectual chops, temperament, experience, humility, ambition—and above all, a capacity for reason.

When they are working as they should, universities will not admit Hamas apologists any more than they might admit Holocaust deniers—not because they go beyond acceptable moral or political bounds but because they fall below acceptable intellectual standards. Offensive speech can sometimes have defensible intellectual uses. But praising Hamas as a "liberation" movement is, if not ignorant or stupid, nakedly disingenuous. That Hamas' defenders have gained such a foothold at many universities may say something about the rise of campus radicalism, but it says even more about the decline in academic standards.

That's where the legitimate goal of increasing viewpoint diversity must be tempered by the requirement that diverse views meet basic requirements of rationality, evidence, and the ability to sustain intellectual challenge. Whether our universities retain the capacity to apply those requirements thoughtfully, consistently, evenhandedly, and with the aim of meeting intellectual rather than political tests is an open question.

To sum up: Greater viewpoint diversity on university campuses (and other ideologically monochrome institutions) is a good and important goal—but also, on its simple terms, an inadequate one. Viewpoint diversity should not just mean the presence of differing opinions on a campus or some other setting; those opinions must be made to engage productively with one another. The ultimate justification for this engagement of views isn't that it furthers the cause of representation; it's that it abets the pursuit of truth. And even as it's usually helpful to have a wider diversity of opinions, there's a limit to how wide they should go: Views that fall below basic intellectual standards don't deserve admission in the community of reason, reasonableness, and good faith.

Which brings me back to my original question: Was I right to turn down a debate about the wisdom and morality of Zionism with my erstwhile sparring partner?

The argument that I was wrong comes to this: Like a tumor, a bad idea will metastasize if allowed to grow unchallenged and uncontradicted. Viewpoint diversity introduces a range of opinions that can shrink, if not destroy, those bad ideas, at least when given the opportunity to engage them. At the same time, an insistence on viewpoint diversity can give good ideas a chance to win wider acceptance, even when initially they are unpopular and held by a tiny few. The role of a university or any other institution that cares about ideas is to widen the space in which various ideas can encounter, learn from, collide, and compete with one another. To narrow that space by decreeing certain ideas beyond the pale does not stop those ideas—if anything, it facilitates their growth. Worse, it creates a basis for others to deem *your* ideas beyond the pale, balkanizing and impoverishing intellectual life as a whole.

But that's not the whole story, at least in this case. In a dim light, it may have been understandable to make the case prior to October 7 that Israeli Jews would be better served living as equal citizens with Palestinians in a binational state. That was at least an argument worth having, because to some American Jews, particularly younger ones, it seemed plausible in theory. But the slaughter of October 7 made vivid, as never before, the misery and murder that would await Jews in Israel if they lost or abandoned their state. And the worldwide rise of raw, proud, and violent anti-semitism that erupted after October 7 also made clear that Jews should not expect safety elsewhere. To call now for the end of Israel invites the destruction of the Jews.

That's not a position that deserves a stage, particularly when it isn't even made forthrightly. It fails the test of intellectual seriousness and honesty. And while there's a case to be made for challenging it (if only to expose it), there is an equal case to be made for ignoring it, especially when what it mainly seeks is notoriety. There is no shortage of discomfiting and intelligent debates to be had in good faith regarding Israel and its future. Proposing that Israel should have no future isn't one of them.

So, was I right or wrong? I'm still not sure. The purpose of this essay is to see both sides of the argument clearly—a reminder, perhaps, that viewpoint diversity exists not only among us, but sometimes, also, within us.

Notes

1 Jesse Singal, "Did I Publish The Private Medical Records Of Transgender Children?," Singal-Minded, Substack, December 12, 2024, https://jessesingal.substack.com/p/did-i-publish-the-private-medical.

2 Carole Hooven, "Why I Left Harvard," The Free Press, January 16, 2024, https://www.thefp.com/p/carole-hooven-why-i-left-harvard?fbclid=IwAR2OIskRiGtX98JyOwLxvvJlOvnWrhU33l2YIflFV37c1P_oSt1dQmwASA0.

Viewpoint Diversity Won't Work, Unless . . .

by Mark Bauerlein

Viewpoint diversity has a special appeal to the many thousands of academics who've been in meetings and discussions over the years with people who reject any alternative thinking about the matter at hand. The encounters have been unpleasant and sometimes included a rebuke or two, the dogmatists in the room making a dissenter feel guilty merely for having raised a challenge, however mildly. I bet many individuals who've joined Heterodox Academy and other outside-the-Establishment groups have undergone the experience. They opened their mouths to wonder about a political slant inserted into a job search, or they suggested a visiting speaker who's pro-life or anti-DEI, or some such proposal that did anything short of affirming campus orthodoxy, and they were chastised for doing so. The response stung and lingered.

We shouldn't underestimate this interpersonal element in the promotion of a wide range of acceptable opinion. I would rate it a motive stronger than ideology or academic freedom. Academics are largely free agents, at least in the softer fields, where they run their own classes and pursue their scholarship alone. Policy disputes within a school or department take time and energy, not to mention producing discomfort among the modest and retiring types. They'd rather skip them and get back to their own tasks.

Sometimes, however, they have to come together to decide matters such as a tenure case, a curriculum change, or the fate of a student, where strong feelings come into play. This is the moment illiberal attitudes do the most damage. They operate potently in collective settings where the enforcement of dogma takes place in front of an audience and adds a concession factor (or disgrace potential) to the colloquy. Apostles of political correctness are fired up; such decisions have long-term consequences; an open debate is a dangerous allowance. The dogmatists share a righteous premise: Why should offensive opinions be granted a platform? They may or may not realize that the attribution of iniquity to the nonconformist is a humiliation for him and distress for the rest—it doesn't matter. They get their way and others leave the room hoping not to return soon. As I said, these feelings don't pass quickly, and the moderates in the department know it can happen again.

It's easy to see how viewpoint diversity is the antidote to this dynamic. Conscientious professors have to deliberate with colleagues, administrators, and students, some of whom are, indeed, rigid and commanding, and they don't like it. Most academics are reasonable, collegial personalities who prefer to avoid open conflict of the very kind forced upon them by doctrinaires. They're unhappy with the bullying and want it to stop. Viewpoint diversity gives them a middle way, a non-confrontational position. It doesn't argue substantively against the contentions of the bullies. It only asks that people have the right to voice a disagreement without shame. There is an epistemology underlying viewpoint diversity, but it doesn't affect the truth of the doctrines that are being pushed, only the aggression with which they are enforced. Richard Rorty described it this way:

> . . . in the process of playing vocabularies and cultures off against each other, we produce new and better ways of talking and acting—not better by reference to a

> previously known standard, but just better in the sense that they come to *seem* clearly better than their predecessors. (*Consequences of Pragmatism*, xxxvii)

The specific wording here is important. The term "playing" suggests debate without rancor; the absence of a "previously known standard" opens the playing to fresh perspectives; and "*seems* clearly better" instead of "*is* clearly better" acknowledges that future revisions to those "better ways" are always possible. Discussion proceeds, progress happens. This is viewpoint diversity at work, though Rorty didn't use the term. No dogma can shut down the exchange and no dogmatist can rule out a contrary voice before it receives a proper hearing (so long as that voice respects academic norms).

This is what makes viewpoint diversity a winning approach: It's a soft resistance to the hard-cases. Viewpoint diversity has no positive content in itself—which is precisely the point. It's nonthreatening, except, of course, to the control freaks in the room whom nobody likes anyway. Advocates see it as a release from intimidation. Many years ago, while in graduate school, I attended a seminar in which a visiting speaker, a genial British fellow, presented a paper entitled "Male Feminism" which laid out ways men in the academy could assume a feminist mantle without undermining female leadership of the movement. A formal respondent was chosen in advance, a feminist scholar of English Romanticism. After he finished his summation of the paper, which had already been distributed, the feminist proceeded with a fifteen-minute dissection of the argument so packed with contempt and condescension that when she finished, the audience remained uncomfortably silent and the speaker stumbled through a few feeble defenses. He'd said the wrong thing, period. What started out as a generous, if clumsy intent by a man to join in the academic recognition of women turned into a "You-don't-know-what-you're-talking-about-so-be-quiet" reproof. A professional lesson was given: Be very careful, this topic is a minefield.

In thirty years as a professor, I witnessed many such occasions, and I'm ashamed to admit the numerous times I failed to step up and speak out. I felt the peril and kept my head down. At a meeting at Dartmouth of American Studies professors that I attended just after earning tenure, a speaker spent five minutes criticizing a renowned American scholar only to have the host of the conference note that the object of his attack was one of the first openly homosexual academics in America, and that the presentation smacked of gay-bashing. I did sense a personal animus in the speaker, but nothing relative to the famed professor's sexuality. Nevertheless, the speaker apologized and squirmed and denied any such intention. Later, when I mentioned the moment to another young attendee, she called the accusation "disgusting" and I agreed—but we had both remained silent. Homosexuality was another one of those delicate topics you'd best avoid if you didn't adopt the sanctioned stand.

Those episodes should never have happened. They are What viewpoint diversity is intended to prevent. It overcomes such reticence as we had shown precisely because of its modesty. It lets the dogmatists have their say, then politely opens the floor to contrarians. You don't have to fight the illiberal ones, only insist that all (suitably academic) voices be heard. Who could argue with that?

There is a problem, however, and it stems precisely from the ostensible advantage of the approach. The problem is this: What do viewpoint-diversiphiles do about colleagues and other campus dwellers who renounce and defy viewpoint diversity? Let's say you have a department of twenty-five members, one of whom is a conservative of some kind, twenty-one of whom are liberal and pluralistic, and three who are inflexible identity politicians. Those three live out their politics avidly; they believe that academic jobs are fundamentally political. They never vote to hire any candidate except one just like themselves. They train graduate students in the same way, rejecting those who don't toe a party line. They show their disgust in department meetings when things don't work out as they demand. They're ideologues, and they aim to make the department in their image.

I'm not exaggerating. In my area of the humanities, the progressivist minority has made remarkable advances. They've inserted diversity statements into job applications, engineered admissions against whites and Asians, promoted identity politics in programs, research, and peer review, and broken the traditional humanities curriculum into multicultural incoherence. The old Ivory Tower norms mean nothing to them; they disdain the ideal of objectivity. One has to respect them for their passion, but their actions are precisely why the call for viewpoint diversity is necessary.

Given their ardor for affirmative action, anti-heteronormativity, diversity on the syllabus, and other dogmas, the principled humility of viewpoint diversity appears outgunned. Everything the dogmatists do runs against the principle, but what means does viewpoint diversity have to stop them other than a final vote? Viewpoint-diversiphiles can't shut them down from opinionating and politicking, for that would contradict viewpoint-diversity rule number one. They know, too, that ideologues dislike the word "Stop." Tensions would rise, producing the very discomfort viewpoint diversity was supposed to reduce. A few years ago, a Stanford history professor wrote an article entitled "The Whitesplaining of History Is Over," which began,

> When the academy was the exclusive playground of white men, it produced the theories of race, gender, and Western cultural superiority that underwrote imperialism abroad and inequality at home. (*Chronicle of Higher Education* 3 Apr 2018).

Does anyone expect an academic so eager to trash her senior white colleagues for their bigotry to welcome other perspectives just because a few moderates in the room ask her to do so? Even if a few people raised evidence against the assertion, it wouldn't affect the animus behind it. It would be nice if viewpoint-diversiphiles were battling only an intellectual position. But there's a psychopolitical condition that must be overcome, too, a zeal and a righteousness, and viewpoint diversity doesn't supply the tools. In the end, academics who espouse pluralism must accept anti-pluralists in their ranks, people who labor daily in opposition to pluralistic ethics.

It's the old liberal dilemma of how much intolerance we must tolerate. If the dogmatists remained a tiny fraction of the whole, with minor impact, perhaps we wouldn't have to fret. But the impact isn't insignificant—it's everywhere. And from what I've seen in humanities departments over the decades, the portion of ideologues hasn't been contained. It's grown. Those three tenured radicals in 1990 became six in 1997, ten in 2005 . . . fully enough to run the department as they wished. The institutional dynamic favored the never-compromising extremists over the sometimes-compromising moderates. This happened because the pluralists in the department exercised their pluralism now and then by agreeing to hire a leftist job candidate, not realizing that the hire would join the minority and be just as rigid. Each time that happened, the ideological climate of the department shifted, though not enough to alarm the moderates. After thirty years, though, work was complete, Woke had triumphed, pluralism was gone.

To reverse the decay of pluralism, viewpoint-diversiphiles must exert their principles more firmly and accept the very confrontations that the approach was geared to avert. They must maintain their principles but enforce them with as much fervor as the dogmatists do theirs. Example: If in a hiring committee meeting a colleague objects to a candidate on political grounds of some kind, one must halt the proceedings and declare, "Political criteria have no place in this —they are a violation of academic freedom—we judge on academic strengths and weaknesses alone. If we move forward this way, I shall file a complaint with the administration."

I know that sounds reactive, but such misbehavior must be met head-on. Other such occasions should evoke similar objections every time. The faculty handbook and, in some cases, state law back the objector. He's right, they're wrong. The only reason the dogmatists have been so brazen in their bias is that nobody has told them so. Their coercions have continued for so long that they have acquired the status of standard operating procedure. They impress some as disciplinary norms. That elevation is fragile, though. A staunch reminder of Ivory Tower objectivity by one willing to accept the sour looks of a few colleagues can topple it. Viewpoint diversity is a necessary but insufficient instrument of academic reform. We need strong men and women, people who bristle at intimidation, who see right through the manipulations and guilt trips of the dogmatists and cry out, "Enough." No more attempts at collegiality with people of "My way or the highway." Higher education cannot proceed unless supporters of pluralism restrain the strident voices of political dogma and insist at every moment in the life of a department "e pluribus unum."

Viewpoint Diversity in the Age of AI

by Hollis Robbins

Every essay in this volume is written on the assumption that viewpoint diversity is a human project. We need more conservatives in law schools, more heterodoxies in classrooms, more pluralism in publishing houses. The shared anxiety is that too many people are silencing too many other people. But what if that entire frame is already outdated? The age of human scarcity, the world where diverse voices are rare and need to be protected, has become a world where synthetic voices are crowding out the human. Viewpoint diversity expressed by individuals in the classroom is still possible in this new world, but only if we are mindful of the ways in which AI shifts the whole landscape of what it means to have a viewpoint and to express it. This essay will provide two viewpoints on the topic of viewpoint diversity in the age of AI: The first is that "generated" diversity is a non-trivial complication for faculty working to broaden the range of views discussed in the classroom; the second is that AI may very well help broaden student views outside the classroom. A new challenge for faculty will be to allow students space and privacy to "try on" views that may well have been AI-generated, if the "trying on" is indeed the pedagogical goal.

The New AI Normal

The AI "viewpoint on demand" problem is already with us. Students can sit in the classroom with a phone under the table, tapping one-thumbed as adept young people do, to ask their generative AI app what to say and from what perspective. Any student at any time can offer a serviceable counterpoint to any line of questioning, complete with supporting data. "What would a climate skeptic say in response to this argument?" Ten words will yield five hundred to please the professor, enliven classroom discussion, and position the student as thoughtful and informed. But what exactly is being achieved in that moment: a student's mind broadened, or the professor's sense of accomplishment?

Putting aside the pressing and serious concerns about AI structural biases, about guardrails too high or too low, about labeling ideas as "harmful," about "safety protocols"—the fact of the matter is that without raising alarms, Large Language Models (LLMs) participate in our public discourse without any intrinsic viewpoint at all. An LLM does not "believe," it predicts. Its outputs are weighted averages of prior expressions. As I have written, the signifiers are not attached to real-world signifiers. LLMs speak in a smooth rhetorical style that seems substantial but is in fact feather light.

Mill did not foresee this contestant in the marketplace of ideas, an entity that thinks like the architect of the market, that builds the stalls, prints the currency, and floods the booths with counterfeits. To call its outputs "viewpoints" is a category mistake.

And yet, these non-viewpoints now flood the arena. At a keystroke, one can summon a Marxist interpretation, a Burkean reflection, a skeptical interjection, a feminist rejoinder without actually "inhabiting" or truly personifying any such stance. In this not-so-brave new world, dissent is cheapened, detached from human cost and human responsibility, and, as such, AI dissent isn't even dissent. It is part of the data set. AI's ability to supply the illusion of heterodoxy in the absence of genuine conviction is a feature, not a bug.

A professor can certainly keep phones and laptops out of the classroom to keep students from typing "what's a libertarian response to universal basic income?" in order to be ready when called upon. But outside the classroom, the easy access to multiple viewpoints can lead to blandness or easy access to the unfamiliar. Most generative systems are tuned toward the plausible middle, smoothing eccentric edges, converging on the statistically median phrase. Answers are pleasing, even when asked for a "feminist" or "authoritarian" perspective. They are calm. They are palatable and "probable." AI can be asked to give three counterarguments to every paper and slot them in seamlessly. Students are already doing this.

But we already know that students and faculty recite platitudes with ease. For decades, surveys by HxA and others have captured student voices admitting, "I never say what I really think in class; I just say what everyone thinks should be said in response." Now, generative AI can help that student express a wide range of viewpoints (let's say it's a previously "suppressed" view of guns or marriage or religion or immigration). The student may or may not hold these views but AI can make them sound reasonable and offer data to back them up. The question is, is this an improvement?

Students are living in a world where dissent is manufactured for everyone. Websites and social media spin up "reader voices" that are angry, sympathetic, contrarian, all fake. The illusion of a robust public square is already upon us and has been for some time. Even when there are "real" readers to supply diverse reactions, the system is ready to augment them. Nobody in this volume wants a pluralism that is ventriloquism, but that is the reality online. A story that is essentially a dozen opinions on one data point is still a story about one data point, but few notice this.

We hear of think tanks "war-gaming" AI-generated "stakeholder comments" in regulatory hearings: simulated farmers, small business owners, environmental advocates, all speaking in the tones of their supposed constituencies. It all looks like broad consultation. And there are fears of the automation of constituency itself.

How Viewpoint Diversity Advocates Might Respond

If the very category of "viewpoint" is shifting under our feet, how do we continue the defense of pluralism that animates this book? I do not pretend to have a full program but let me suggest a few directions.

First, we must name and preserve the human stakes. If we believe there is something irreplaceable about a person standing behind an idea, not just the idea, let's protect the person as well as the idea. When a student hazards an unpopular opinion, when a journalist signs her name to a column, when a citizen testifies at a hearing, there is a cost, a responsibility, a mark of authorship. To care about viewpoint diversity among people, not among ideas, we must make clear the difference between a view that is held and one that is generated.

One response might be that if students or professionals can now summon a contrarian argument in two seconds, deliberative settings should reward reflection, not latency. The idea might be structuring debates where participants must sit with an opposing view for a week before responding, or requiring engagement with identifiable sources rather than machine composites.

Others in this volume defend slowness. One contributor insists that "in the classroom, the most important thing a teacher can do is leave silence after the question, allowing dissent to gather the courage to be spoken." Another reminds us that "constitutional rights are safeguarded precisely because courts move at a slower rhythm than the passions of the moment." Another writes that "publishing should resist the churn of social media and preserve the longer cycle of drafting, review, and revision." These are all recognitions of the value of delay: that democracy, scholarship, and teaching depend on intervals where nothing happens outwardly, but much happens inwardly.

I want to call that value latency. Latency is not dead time but thinking time, the pause between stimulus and response in which a human being wrestles with an idea, risks being wrong, tests language against conviction. It is in latency that responsibility attaches to a viewpoint. An AI can produce an answer in two seconds, but that is only technical latency; it lacks the drag of thought. Human latency is the work and space where disagreement is tried on, inhabited, rejected. Students may be doing this with their ChatGPTs. They may be doing this more than we are aware.

Another response might be to expose students to a broad range of views through reading archival documents that AI does not have access to. If we believe the classroom should include the jagged, the offensive, the troubling, let's foreground complicated authentic voices from past eras, however uncomfortable, to show the depth of division and the difficulty of change. There is great benefit in showing diversity rather than eliciting it. Students may respond by uploading archival documents into their AI models and grappling with them there, asking for context and explanations, but even this would be an example of students engaging with diverse materials.

My point is that there is a risk in stating that counterfeit diversity is no diversity at all. While it is true that synthetic voices carry no risk, no courage, no accountability, the access to a machine that can produce both sides of every argument could be a tool toward pluralism, just one that the professor will not necessarily see. Students can swiftly get an answer in class but they may also noodle casually with their AI in their rooms, over long periods of time, in ways that result in unexpected ideas being planted, just not by the professor or fellow students.

There is a danger in the age of AI that professors may leap to the conclusion that for viewpoint diversity to be meaningful, it must involve genuine human engagement, that the person speaking must genuinely hold the view, is "grappling" with it, or is "changing their mind." Calls for civic grace still assume an environment where participants' thoughts are open for scrutiny.

Even in the cancel culture days, I was concerned about demand for intellectual transparency about one's private convictions. Sometimes one prefers to be silent for reasons other than fear.

That is, advocates of both orthodoxy and heterodoxy can seem overly concerned with the inner lives of others. Campus activists, literary gatekeepers, political pundits are regularly diagnosing "real" motives. Utterances are captured, preserved, dissected. The marketplace is filled with amateur mind-readers.

In the work of separating the human "viewpoint" from an AI-generated one, faculty should take care not to invade a student's privacy. There's a space between an AI-generated proposition and seeing the statement as a direct window into the speaker's soul. There's a way that a student might want to use ChatGPT rather than worry that the professor and fellow students will be prying into their head and drawing conclusions based on a viewpoint expressed simply to see how it sounds or felt to say it. One has the right to participate in a public intellectual exercise without surrendering private thoughts to scrutiny. Faculty should understand that a student arguing with ChatGPT at home may be engaging in viewpoint diversity far from the classroom.

I worry that the professor who wants to "draw out" quiet students is seeking a performance of a student's inner struggle for the benefit of the class. I worry that the call for "confident pluralism" or "speaking from your particularity" presupposes a willingness to make one's private convictions public as the price of admission to the conversation. Practices of self-censorship might not always be about fear of cancellation but about the desire to be left alone. A student and a professor have a right to a private, inaccessible inner world. One has the right to try on an argument like a coat, to see how it fits, without anyone assuming it is now part of one's skin.

In this light, students using ChatGPT may not be lazy and may not be cowards. They may simply want to express a thought without having to stand for it. Generative AI, for these students, becomes a tool to defend their mind against the demand for transparency. The classroom is not a confessional.

The arrival of generative AI and synthetic voices could be thought of as the social and logical endpoint of a culture that has destroyed intellectual privacy. Many people seem to prefer asking a machine to asking a person. The proliferation of campus chatbots for financial aid, housing, course selection, and advising show this to be true. If schools, particularly, have created a demand for constant, authentic self-revelation, why shouldn't young people be eager to seek refuge behind machine-generated shields? LLMs don't judge and they don't have an agenda beyond answering each prompt.

The defenders of viewpoint diversity in this volume share a commitment to human flourishing through intellectual encounter. AI forces us to clarify what we mean by "human" in that equation. It is not enough to have warm bodies in the room if those bodies are merely conduits for machine-generated content. But neither should we respond by demanding that students (or professors) bare their souls as proof of authenticity. The path forward requires creating spaces where genuine human thinking can occur, spaces that protect both the labor of thought and the privacy of the thinker. Only then can we distinguish between diversity that enriches human understanding and diversity that merely populates databases. In an age of synthetic voices, the right of humans to think privately may be the precondition for thinking at all.

II

Viewpoint Diversity in Society and Politics

The Paradox of Infinite Voices and Narrow Minds

by Yascha Mounk

The year 2025 is a strange time to worry about viewpoint diversity. In the palm of my hand, I am holding a smart phone which gives me access to a greater diversity of views than has perhaps ever before been available to humans. On social media apps, in podcasts followed by millions of people, and increasingly even in traditional media, I can follow people who argue for communism and for fascism, listen to them making the case for social justice or for Islamic theocracy, or seek out those who will urge me to become a Catholic monk or a Hassidic Jew.

Since the large-scale deployment of artificial intelligence, I can even ask ChatGPT or Grok or DeepSeek to state whatever argument I choose in the tones and the style of any moral tradition that takes my fancy. John Stuart Mill famously argued that it is crucial to hold our beliefs as living truths rather than dead dogmas, something that would only be possible if we were exposed to a genuine diversity of views. "If opponents of all important truths do not exist," he suggested, "it is indispensable to imagine them and supply them with the strongest arguments which the most skillful devil's advocate can conjure up." Today, that devil's advocate is accessible to any human with an internet connection.

And yet, the unprecedented diversity of viewpoints that is now available to—and to some extent inescapable for—the citizens of modern democracies coexist with a greater homogeneity of thought in key spheres of civil society than has been characteristic of life in the West in any historical epoch since the Victorian period. If you are an artist or an academic or a social worker or a psychologist—or, increasingly, a journalist or doctor or lawyer or civil servant—you likely operate in a social milieu in which the range of respectable opinion is strikingly narrow.

Oddly, that adherence to a narrow band of opinion is largely self-imposed. There are (at least in the United States—the story is sadly rather different in much of Europe) no formal legal constraints on expressing a different point of view. The modes of censorship that leading social media companies, in clandestine cooperation with the state, imposed for the past decade have largely disappeared. There is even a good living in refusing to toe that line: You can accumulate a lot of fame and perhaps ascend to the highest echelons of political power by assailing those respectable nostrums, turning yourself into an angry pundit. But if you happen to be a normie professional who simply wants to enjoy a good career and a peaceful life, the incentive to pay lip service to a list of narrow articles of faith remains overwhelming.

Homogeneity breeds conformity. Because many of these professions are now so dominated by people with one point of view, the rising generation of professionals tends to share the same worldview. And where the conformity isn't genuine, coercion can create its appearance. Surveys reveal that an astonishing share of people in a broad range of professions regularly engage in self-censorship.

I have come to think of this strange coexistence between an unprecedented variety of opinions that are strongly represented in the public square and the rigid worldview that constrains the beliefs of the most influential people in our society as the paradox of infinite voices and narrow minds. Never before have so many opinions been at our fingertips—and never before have so many professionals felt unable to voice theirs. What explains this paradox, why does it matter, and what can we do about it?

The Brooklynization of the Bourgeoisie

It is impossible to understand the recent politics of the western world without considering a giant sociological transformation—one that, inevitable though it may seem in retrospect, nearly nobody predicted: The bourgeoisie has switched sides.

For much of the nineteenth and twentieth centuries, the proletariat was the political stronghold of the left. The bourgeoisie was the stronghold of the right. Indeed, the assumption that affluent professionals would tend to be conservative is reflected in the most famous political treatises and pieces of art that the period produced.

Karl Marx called on the workers, not on the schoolteachers or freelance illustrators, of the world to unite. The origins of Germany's Social Democratic Party, of Britain's Labour Party, and even of the modern-day Democratic Party in the United States lies with factory workers and trade unionists. In Jacques Brel's song "Les Bourgeois," three young men mock the conservative pieties of their elders by mooning the notaries of a small French town; when, by song's end, the protagonists, themselves now middle-aged notaries, are mooned in turn, the obvious implication is that they too have turned into conservatives.

But of late, these realities have started to shift, with huge impacts on contemporary politics. It is astonishing, for example, that according to *The Economist*, the socio-economic profile of the coalition assembled by Kamala Harris, the Democratic presidential candidate in 2024, most closely resembles the socio-economic profile of the coalition assembled by Bob Dole, the Republican presidential candidate, in 1996. (Unsurprisingly, both lost.)

This transformation is even visible in the realm of popular culture. Take, as an example, the most famous American cartoon of the last decades. When *The Simpsons* first aired, Homer Simpson was likely a Democrat, his pious neighbor Ned Flanders definitely a Republican. But over the three decades that the show has been on air, the nature of America's partisan divide has shifted so much that any politically astute viewer would now assume these characters to have rather different loyalties. Flanders may be sufficiently alienated by the coarseness of the populist right to vote for the Democrats; Homer would undoubtedly support Donald Trump.

This transformation has been called by a variety of names. Thomas Piketty has described it as the rise of the Brahmin left. David Brooks has written about the rise of the Bobo. Matthew Yglesias has lamented the rise of The Groups. I propose to call it the Brooklynization of the Bourgeoisie: New York's wealthy used to live on the Upper East Side, to pride themselves in their old family ties, to value markers of high culture like the opera, and to vote conservative; today, they live in Brooklyn, believe that they have earned their place in the upper echelons of society thanks to succeeding in a meritocratic competition, are more likely to care about rock bands or microbrews, and think of themselves as progressive.

That same transformation also helps to explain the Paradox of Infinite Voices and Narrow Minds. The population of the United States, and of many other western democracies, is now deeply stratified by educational achievement. The affluent and highly credentialed are mostly on the political left. The working class is increasingly drifting to the political right. And that has deeply transformed the composition, the values, and even the actions of the professional class.

Plumbers are right wing but lawyers are left wing. Cab drivers are right wing but university professors are left wing. Police officers are right wing but civil servants are left wing. And though many professions claim to be apolitical, the plumbers and cab drivers and police officers increasingly suspect that the lawyers and professors and civil servants are letting their political values influence their work. The decline in respect for "experts" is in part owed to the blatant lies spread on social media; but it also has its roots in the real ways in which the consensus within these professions has increasingly come to adhere to a narrowly progressive—and often lamentably erroneous—set of assumptions about the world.

The Brooklynization of the Bourgeoisie also has another side effect. Lawyers, university professors, and civil servants have outsized influence on the rules, norms, and decisions that structure a lot of day-to-day life. And that leaves many less-affluent and less-educated citizens feeling that the democracy they were promised is a sham. "We are the majority," they complain, "but no one listens to us anyway."

The resulting state of affairs leaves both sides equally unhappy. Many citizens feel ignored, besieged, and detested by a professional class which believes that it is entitled to rule, and finds the views of many of their compatriots intolerably bigoted. That is of great political significance because, even in highly affluent countries, there are more plumbers, cab drivers, and police officers than there are lawyers, university professors, and civil servants. Meanwhile, members of the professional class feel bewildered at the lack of respect for their expertise, and fearful that the barbarians at the political gates will soon come for their heads.

What one side perceives as flagrantly unjust domination by the well-credentialed, the other interprets as the perils of revanchist demagoguery.

Barbarians Inside the Gate

Largely unnoticed by the combatants in an increasingly ferocious culture war, both of these impressions are rooted in reality. Seemingly rival to each other, they actually make up a coherent whole—as the transformation of an important, and sometimes oddly overlooked, group of professionals demonstrates.

There is one group of professionals that I have so far omitted to mention: elected officials. These officials differ from other upper middle-class professionals because voters ostensibly select them for their political views. But in sharp contrast to the past, when many of them, especially on the left, had working-class backgrounds, nearly all of them have also undergone an extensive process of socialization as middle-class professionals. With few exceptions, elected officials in the United States, in the United Kingdom, and most of continental Europe, have attended universities, spent long periods of time living in big urban centers of economic opportunity, perhaps worked in fields like the law, media, or academia, and now make upper middle-class wages. If it looks like a professional, talks like a professional, and earns like a professional, then it is probably a professional—with all the cultural and ideological accoutrements that nowadays come with that status.

It should, then, come as no surprise that, as a recent paper by Laurenz Günther shows, a significant gap has formed between the views of elected officials and those of the voters they are supposed to represent. In Germany in 2013, a time when right-wing populists had not yet made it into the national parliament, for example, the average politician was much more likely than the average voter to say that it should be easier to immigrate to the country. In fact, even the average member of the Bundestag for the Christian Democrats, the most right-leaning party to be represented in that body at that time, was well to the left of the median voter on this question.

Similar gaps of political representation, Günther shows, also held in other countries and for other topics. They are evident in questions about how severe the sentences for violent criminals should be; in questions about whether schools should teach students to obey social authorities; and in questions about whether politicians should prioritize the fight against climate change over economic growth.

There are many partial explanations for the astonishing success of populist parties over the past decade. The rise of the internet and of social media, for example, clearly made it easier for outsiders to storm the political stage and intensified the public's tendency to see the world in unremittingly negative terms. But as Günther suggests, the big gap in views about cultural topics between most voters and most of their representatives surely played an important role: The most straightforward reason why right-wing populists have gained so much in vote share of late "is that they fill the cultural representation gap."

The lack of viewpoint diversity in important professions does real harm to their ability to deliver on their mission. A psychologist who prioritizes the abstract demands of social justice over the well-being of the patient sitting in front of him in his office fails to live up to his duty of healing patients. A social scientist who is so afraid of what her colleagues might say about her latest study if its findings happen to run counter to some sacred article of faith fails to live up to her duty of advancing human knowledge. But these kinds of harms, well-chronicled by other contributions to this volume, only capture the most immediate impact of the Brooklynization of the Bourgeoisie. Its ultimate harm stems from the representation gap that has opened up between ordinary citizens and those calling the shots in society—and the counterproductive rebellion it inspired.

How Not to MAGA

Populists are able to win power in good part because they promise their voters that they will do what they can to close this representation gap. Legislators, they say, will finally start listening to the views of the people. Professions that have been captured by ideologues enforcing a narrow orthodoxy will be forced to become more representative. Institutions which once had disdain for ordinary people will finally feel their wrath.

There are real reasons why these promises have proven so enticing. Anybody who completely dismisses that this anger is based in real failings of the professional elite is refusing to grapple seriously with this political moment. And yet, the record of populists in India and Turkey, in Hungary and Venezuela suggests that these promises are rarely fulfilled—and the first months of Donald Trump's second administration in the United States only serve to reinforce that suspicion.

When populists rise to power, they tend to assail institutions that have lost the trust of the population. In the United States, for example, Donald Trump has exploited the unpopularity of universities like Harvard and Columbia by subjecting them to an unprecedented assault from the federal government. The ostensible purpose of this assault was to right the ways in which they had become inhospitable to opinions which violated rigid campus orthodoxies. And in certain particulars, those complaints really were well-founded. It is now, for example, well-documented that the mandatory diversity statements which many universities used in their hiring practices over the course of the past decade in practice forced applicants to pay lip service to the mantras of critical race theory (with anybody who refused to comply excluded from serious consideration).

But it has also quickly become obvious that the White House was never truly interested in broadening the range of views which would be permissible, or even those that would be commonly represented, on the nation's most prestigious college campuses. Instead, it seems to have two goals, which may stand in slight tension with each other, but are equally inimical to the true cause of viewpoint diversity.

To the extent possible, recent executive orders and other administrative actions by the White House have sought to replace one set of dogmas with another. Instead of pushing back against the forms of ideological coercion which do persist, they have simply created a new set of do's and don'ts. If it was previously taboo to criticize the nostrums of critical race theory, a raft of new laws, executive orders, and administrative fiats attempt to stifle academics who teach these ideas. And instead of mandating that virtually all research must in some way promote the cause of diversity, public funding bodies have indiscriminately cut grants which commit the faux pas of mentioning such terms in any way—in the most absurd cases, even if they used them in a wholly unpolitical context.

At the same time, the White House also seems to have recognized that no amount of pressure from the federal government will transform the ideological leanings of most faculty at leading universities. And so, its recent activity appears to aim as much at weakening as at transforming these institutions. The point is not to change the culture at institutions which populists rightly recognize as hostile to their worldview; increasingly, it is to weaken the power bastion of their ideological adversary at any cost.

From a purely partisan adversary, this is probably a shrewd judgment. The cynics in the White House who have concluded that the cause of the MAGA movement is better served by besieging than by reforming universities may be right about how difficult it would be for legislative fiat to undo the long-term effects of a much deeper sociological transformation of the professional class. But anybody who cares about preserving institutions that actually allow a broad range of people to do science, to argue about the world, and to criticize the powerful in honest and intelligent terms should be appalled by what is being sacrificed in the process. To undermine the great contributions that the United States has made in fields from computing to neuroscience in the service of undermining the department of comparative literature is both bad for humanity and for anybody who genuinely aspires to make America great again.

Diversity of Institutions (Within and Between)

It is hard to see a quick way out of the Paradox of Infinite Voices and Narrow Minds. This political moment increasingly resembles a Greek tragedy whose protagonists, unable to grasp the larger forces that determine their actions, are quickly gaining ground on the abyss. The professionals whose values are so far out of keeping with those of the rest of the population and the populists who are promising to use all the power they can amass to let the will of the people prevail see each other as mortal enemies; what neither seems to grasp is that they are actually one another's biggest assets. And whoever ends up winning, it is the goal of viewpoint diversity—and the deeper values, like freedom of speech and freedom of conscience, with which it is intimately intertwined—which is likely to perish as a result.

The technological forces which have allowed such a great variety of viewpoints to enter the public square are unlikely to subside. The sociological transformations which have created a professional class beholden to an ideologically narrow set of nostrums is unlikely to reverse. And the populists who have been empowered by the resulting gap between the actions of key social institutions and the views of ordinary people are, despite their promises, likely to keep limiting true diversity of viewpoints in their own ways. It's easy to see how things could go from bad to worse.

For the most part, the solution to this narrow problem hinges on the solution to a much broader set of problems. Institutions that want to sustain broad legitimacy must recall that they should be more beholden to their founding missions than to the ideological predilections of their members. This applies to institutions from Harvard to NPR and from the Ford Foundation to Coca-Cola. It also, of course, applies to political parties: If mainstream parties cared deeply about basic constitutional values, and were able to close the cultural representation gap, they would leave much less oxygen for demagogues who blithely reject those values.

There is, however, one more direct change that advocates of viewpoint diversity can try to bring about in the meantime: One of the reasons why a diversity of viewpoints could so quickly have eroded within the professional world has to do with the fact that there has been a concerted attack on the ability to express different opinions in places like Harvard or Columbia, and many of the contributions to this volume rightly focus on that. But another big reason is that there is so little true diversity *between* institutions, with many colleges and law firms and corporations adopting increasingly similar cultures, policies, and operating procedures. And this suggests that one of the partial solutions lies in establishing new institutions that differ radically from the old.

There are over two thousand colleges in the United States. At the lower end of social prestige, there is a great variety of such institutions, from community colleges serving heavily immigrant communities to religious schools preaching the Good News about Jesus. But all the schools at the top range of prestige have over the past decades come to resemble each other to a remarkable degree. However much their respective college tour guides may wax lyrical to visiting high school seniors about their idiosyncratic local traditions, Harvard and Princeton, Yale and Stanford, Duke and Columbia are all examples of what biologists call "convergent evolution." It is not just in the substance of their prevailing views that they constantly copy and emulate each other; it is also in the design of their curricula, in the way they finance their institutions, and in the criteria they use to select their undergraduate class.

The same holds true in many other realms. There are tens of thousands of law firms in the United States. But the culture at the most prestigious, from Cravath to Skadden to Wachtell, is much more similar than that variety might suggest to a naive observer. Even the mainstream press suffers from the same malady, especially when it comes to proudly progressive publications. A few decades ago, there were distinctive differences in style and content between *Dissent*, *The Nation*, and the *New Republic*; a well-versed reader could probably have guessed with a high degree of accuracy which article had appeared in which of these publications. Today, these magazines have largely lost their distinctive identities; just about any article which appears in one of these publications could just as easily appear in another.

The situation is, of course, even worse in those areas in which a single institution holds outsized sway. Top-level researchers in the natural sciences need to plan their research, more or less, in such a way that it meets with the approval of the National Institutes of Health or the National Science Foundation. Psychologists must abide with the dicta of the American Psychological Association. And researchers in global health better make sure that their proposed work fits the agenda of the biggest private philanthropists in the field, such as the Gates Foundation.

It is this tendency towards convergent evolution which makes it so hard to sustain a genuine variety of thought and opinion within the professional class. If one prestigious university applied different standards for admission and hiring than another, if the culture of one law firm radically diverged from that of another, if the journalistic enforcers of ideological orthodoxies still had genuine debates amongst each other, if scientists were not beholden to a tiny number of funding bodies, and if professional associations were less quick to impose their ideological certainties on their members, professionals with dissident—or merely diffident—views would find it much easier to sustain thriving careers and speak their minds.

Thankfully, there are some incipient signs that those professionals who have grown uncomfortable within mainstream institutions, or been cast out for daring to speak up, are starting to organize. Across the country, new universities and alternative media outlets and rival professional associations are forming. It is too early to know whether they will succeed in establishing genuine alternatives to existing structures, and even whether they will actually stick to their ostensible mission of promoting viewpoint diversity. But they are a small green shoot amidst a devastating drought.

The cause of viewpoint diversity remains much imperiled. One of the best ways to serve this embattled cause is to widen our understanding of what its success will require, both now and when the political constellation shall change: true diversity, both within and between institutions. If we want viewpoint diversity, we must not only protect dissenting voices—but also cultivate dissenting institutions.

Pluralism, Particularity, and Possibility

by John Inazu

(The inaugural Duke Pluralism Lecture, March 27, 2025)

The text that follows is taken from the inaugural Pluralism Lecture that I delivered at Duke Chapel in April 2025. I was especially grateful to be asked to be the first speaker for this annual lecture series established at my alma mater twice over—I received my B.S.E. in civil engineering from Duke's Pratt School of Engineering and my law degree from Duke Law School. I chose to focus my Pluralism Lecture on a blend of personal and professional observations that began to emerge during my time at Duke. This particular convergence also points to the importance of place in forming our beliefs and the ways that we engage in a world of difference.

I first set foot in this building thirty-two years ago, when Maya Angelou spoke at the convocation for my freshman class in the fall of 1993. I took the bus over from my freshman dorm, Pegram, grabbed dinner in what was then called The Pits, and nervously began my college experience sitting somewhere in the same pews where you are now. Dr. Angelou asked us to be not just consumers but participants during our time at Duke. As she put it then: "Take responsibility of the time you take up and the space you occupy."

Tonight, I want to explore with you the challenges and opportunities that come from taking Dr. Angelou's charge seriously. When you shift from being passive consumers to engaged participants, you will pay more attention to how you can contribute to the aspirations of this university. This is true not only for students but also for faculty, staff, and administrators. I take it that one of Duke's aspirations, which this new lecture series recognizes, is to be the kind of place that models and cultivates the pluralism necessary to sustain the democratic fabric of our country.

Pluralism is a word with many meanings, so let me give you two definitions I will use tonight. First, pluralism refers to the fact of difference, or the reality that we live in a diverse society. Second, pluralism describes one way that we can respond to that difference.

Let's start with pluralism as the fact of difference. We live in a society deeply divided over things that matter. We disagree over the meaning of human flourishing, the purpose of our country, and what makes a just world. These differences are real, they are deep, and they are not going away. Descriptively, we live in a pluralistic society.

The second definition of pluralism is a political and cultural response to our differences. It's what I have elsewhere called confident pluralism: We learn to live with the differences we don't like, and more importantly, with the people around us who embody those differences.

Confident pluralism requires humility, patience, and tolerance as we navigate our differences. It encourages persuasion rather than coercion in our efforts to convince others why we have the better argument. Confident pluralism is difficult, messy, and imperfect. It is also far better than the alternative. We can rightly critique the many imperfections and injustices in our country and its leaders and still be grateful that we do not resolve our differences with street violence.

I have spent the past decade advocating for the importance of confident pluralism. But I did not have this understanding when

I first arrived at Duke. Tonight, I would like to retrace part of my journey toward confident pluralism. I want to suggest that recognizing our firmly held convictions can help us navigate the deep differences in our pluralistic society. I'll frame my path toward confident pluralism around three themes: particularity, purpose, and perseverance.

Particularity

Let me start with particularity. My story begins, fittingly for this lecture, in the basement of Duke Chapel. As a college sophomore, I joined an interfaith council of undergraduate representatives from various campus ministries: Protestant, Catholic, Jewish, and Muslim, plus a smattering of other groups.

Our interfaith council was well-intentioned but a little naïve. We all wanted civility, community, and good service projects. But our Saturday morning meetings never led us to really know one another—we never learned each other's stories. Instead, we stretched our shared experience of Maya Angelou and Duke basketball into an assumed consensus that never engaged our disagreements about the nature of God, what it means to be a good person, or what happens when you die.

One of the reasons we fell short was a lack of commitment to particularity. Most of us entered the interfaith conversation searching for solidarity instead of exploring our differences. Lacking the tools and vocabulary for genuine interfaith engagement, we looked instead for the lowest common denominator across our faith traditions but made little effort to understand how our differences affected how we saw the world.

If I'm honest, my nineteen-year-old self may have had a little too much particularity. I was sure that my beliefs were correct, and by extension, I was sure that many of those around me were wrong. Confidence in one's faith is not itself a bad thing. But at the time, I lacked the resources to share my own firmly held commitments while also inviting others to share theirs.

This early interfaith experience taught me the importance of particularity in relationships that bridge difference. Our differences matter, and we should not pretend otherwise. But engaging authentically and graciously across differences also means seeking as much as possible to learn why others believe differently. That is the work of empathy. When we commit to this work, we can see how our beliefs and traditions diverge, but we can also discover meaningful common ground—perhaps even more meaningful than basketball. We can discover that you don't have to agree about the nature of God to serve meals at a soup kitchen, or share the same politics to care for hurting neighbors recovering from a hurricane. We can discover that we are all works in progress, we are all fighting our own battles, and we all have blind spots.

Some of us will navigate relationships across differences on our own, but most of us will encounter them through institutions like Duke University. And this brings me to my second point: We engage best across our particularities when we know the purpose of our engagement.

Purpose

The last few years have seen an uptick of college and university initiatives promoting "dialogue across difference." Many of these well-intended efforts offer time-constrained opportunities to meet and talk with someone different from you. But these seldom lead to long-term trust or genuine understanding. Structured dialogue turns out to be very unlike the real world in which we actually encounter differences. People don't usually learn to empathize with one another through dialogue alone—we learn by forming relationships with others committed to a shared endeavor. We build meaningful relationships by working toward endeavors that unite us across our differences. And that requires a sense of purpose.

I learned about the importance of purpose from an unlikely pairing: Stanley Hauerwas and the United States Air Force.

I attended Duke on an ROTC scholarship and stayed for law school before serving four years as an Air Force attorney at the Pentagon. My military service was sandwiched between classes with Hauerwas—a longtime member of the Duke Divinity faculty and a well-known pacifist.

You can imagine that the collision of these influences in my life was not easy to navigate. There is much that I admire about the military, but its emphasis on patriotism and force did not sit easily with someone reading books like *Resident Aliens* and *The Peaceable Kingdom*.

Still, Hauerwas and the military both taught me the importance of purpose: knowing why you are in a particular place and time, with a particular group of people, attempting to do a particular thing. From Hauerwas and related thinkers like Alasdair MacIntyre, I learned that values and virtues unfold within social practices oriented toward specific ends. Purpose brings clarity and coherence to our shared human activities.

Purpose also constrains. It sets the boundaries of acceptable disagreement in any human activity—it sets the limits of pluralism. If a company's purpose is making widgets, its directors may not demand that it make music. If a country's purpose is to advance democracy, its leaders should not promote lawlessness or deny due process. If a university's purpose is to educate, its trustees should not tolerate sophistry.

In the military, I experienced how clarity of purpose unifies by distinguishing relevant differences from irrelevant ones. During basic training, when it was time to scale a wall, nobody cared who you voted for or whether you believed in God. They cared whether you could help them get over the wall. Later, while serving on active duty, my mission to support my fellow servicemembers was similarly clear.

Purpose brings clarity of mission and sets the boundaries of disagreement. Absent purpose, the loudest voices prevail and fear and anxiety triumph over wisdom and judgment. But clarity around purpose can also invite opportunities to learn from differences of perspective and belief. When you know your purpose, you know your boundaries and you know yourself.

I wonder whether Duke University knows its purpose. How, for example, do Duke's pluralistic and educational aspirations fit within its complicated landscape of investments, athletics, and medical care? How does Duke maintain its purpose across its many stakeholders who want it to be many different things? My hope is that amidst these competing pressures, Duke can model a kind of confident pluralism—that it can be the kind of university whose classrooms, laboratories, and faculty lounges welcome progressives and conservatives, religious believers and atheists, Trump voters and Harris supporters—all of whom are themselves committed to a common educational experience. Our country desperately needs such places, and institutions that can name their purpose and therefore the boundaries of their disagreement will be best positioned to become them.

Perseverance

The third and final lesson of my journey toward confident pluralism is perseverance. I owe this lesson to many friends, but tonight I'll focus on one of them, Eboo Patel. Eboo is a Muslim American who founded an organization called Interfaith America, which focuses on navigating religious difference and pluralism across various sectors including higher education. Eboo often observes that elite universities excel at teaching students various identity markers that contribute to diversity in our society—except when it comes to religious differences. But our religious differences underlie some of humanity's deepest and most profound conflicts. How, Eboo asks, can someone be considered an educated citizen of a country founded on principles of religious freedom and toleration without a basic understanding of our religious differences and why they matter? And not just the visually obvious differences of religious attire that make for a good website picture or Instagram post, but the deeper, often incommensurable differences over dietary requirements, worship and prayer, and beliefs about gender and sexuality.

Once we surface our actual differences, we'll need to muddle through learning how to engage with one another across unfamiliar and perhaps even off-putting practices. Eboo and I have muddled through different customs, language norms, and prayer practices. We have learned that friendship across difference requires perseverance. And in our perseverance we have also discovered a great deal of common ground and shared experience: We have taught together, written together, laughed together—we have even been protested together. We have also learned that we have similar dispositions—Eboo likes to joke that it's a good thing we were born in this century; our bookish instincts would not have lasted long in a hunter-gatherer or warrior culture.

Most of the time my religious differences with Eboo do not arise in contentious ways. Many interfaith friendships require greater perseverance. Shared meals where one person's religion requires eating food that another's religion finds unclean. Conferences where one faith requires gender segregation and another strives for gender equality. Partnerships between progressive and conservative believers with different views about the meaning of marriage. These kinds of differences require forbearance, empathy, and forgiveness.

Forgiveness may be the most difficult part of perseverance. Our ability to forgive depends on our ability to see ourselves in need of forgiveness and able to be forgiven. If you think you have never wronged another person, it will be hard to persuade you to forgive the imperfect people who wrong you. On the other hand, if you see yourself as tainted to the point of being unforgivable, you may be unsure of why extending forgiveness to someone else would even matter. For Christians, the Gospel names both the reality of our fallenness and the surety of our forgiveness. As my friend Tim Keller put it, "We are more sinful and flawed in ourselves than we ever dared believe, yet at the very same time we are more loved and accepted in Jesus Christ than we ever dared hope."

That kind of forgiveness plays out in big and small ways, in ordinary friendships and extraordinary injustices. We will need it to persevere in our relationships across difference, where we are going to keep misunderstanding and hurting each other. Come to think of it, that's true not only of our relationships across difference—its true of all our relationships. We can choose to keep our ledgers and exact vengeance whenever we are wronged. Or we can choose to forgive.

My time at Duke began with Maya Angelou. It ended with Jimmy Carter. In his words to our graduating class, President Carter drew from the Apostle Paul and urged us to commit our lives to things unseen: justice, truth, compassion, service, and love. In our deeply divided society, we will argue about the meaning of these words and how best to accomplish them. But we can commit to charity and generosity in the way that we argue. We don't always get to choose our differences, but we can choose how we respond to them.

Possibility

In that spirit, let me leave you with one final word: possibility. Institutions like Duke confront serious challenges in today's landscape of higher education. But I would like to believe that Duke at its core remains a place where teachers and students are engaged in a shared effort to learn together. That it is a place of slow reading and even slower thinking. Unlike the fast-paced world into which most students are headed, I'd like to think that Duke is a place that can lower the stakes and lengthen the conversations.

As I look out at all of you tonight, I'm reminded that pluralism isn't just a theory—it's embodied in the people we meet, the friendships we form, and the institutions that shape us. It's in the courage to hold firm to our own convictions while making room for others to hold theirs. It's in the purpose that binds us across our differences and the perseverance that carries us when understanding and patience run thin. In a world where our deep differences are not going away—where the fact of pluralism increasingly demands a generous and hopeful response rather than a fearful or self-interested one—my hope is that you will choose to join in this difficult, necessary work—with particularity, purpose, and perseverance.

How to Be a Confident Pluralist

by Danielle Allen

While our times are noisy with disagreement, even as too many also shy away from debate, I have always found great life rewards in being a confident pluralist. Over time, I've had occasion to think more deeply about precisely what it means to be a confident pluralist. The theme comes down at its core to a basic question of how we humans relate to one another across differences of viewpoints, beliefs, and identities.

In my book *Talking to Strangers*, I drew on Aristotle to make the case for the virtue of political friendship—being neither domineering in relation to others, nor obsequious, but hitting a middle ground of authentically claiming one's own values and interests, while also charitably and creatively engaging the diverse and various views and interests of others. John Inazu has offered another name for this ethic, i.e. "confident pluralism," in his book *Confident Pluralism: Surviving and Thriving Through Deep Difference* (2016). I adapt this principle here by naming as "confident pluralists" those who are able to live by an ethic of political friendship, treating other humans *as if* they are our friends, regardless of our actual emotional connection, or lack thereof.

This ethic is not just a personal stance—it is also an ethic of citizenship. Civic education, whether in K–12 or higher education, should aim to cultivate citizens who can combine conviction with respect, and who can navigate disagreement without sacrificing either conviction or human dignity. Confident pluralism is one way to name this goal.

The purpose of this essay is to describe what a "confident pluralist" is and then lay out the steps necessary to become such a person.

Family Lessons in Pluralism

I learned what a confident pluralist is from my family. These days, I'm a combination of a Harvard professor and democracy advocate. When people ask me what I work on, I always give the same answer: democracy, past, present, and future, with no question mark at the end of that list. I come by that laser-like focus very honestly, through basic family inheritance.

On my dad's side, my grandfather helped found one of the first NAACP chapters in Northern Florida in the 1940s. They did important work for civil rights and especially for voting rights. Lynchings were on the rise at the time, so my grandfather was taking his life into his own hands to do this work. On my mom's side, my great-grandparents fought for women's suffrage. In 1917, my great-grandfather marched with the suffragettes on Boston Common in a season when women marching in D.C. were being jailed. These were people committed to personal empowerment as the bedrock for human thriving and well-being. And they were all told their goals were impossible. Their answer: These goals are not impossible—they are necessary. The only question is, how will we achieve them?

For many people today, it seems almost impossible to forge bonds across lines of difference, especially differences of political perspective. But that work is necessary, and, once again, the only question is how. The answer to that question has both personal and civic value. My grandfather and other early ancestors were the first examples in my life of confident pluralists, people who knew what mattered to them and why, and who were respectful in their engagements with others about those values, but who were always also moving their cause and purpose forward. They all carried a bright energy of purpose that drew respect from others—the personal reward of a confident pluralist. They all made meaningful differences in their communities, improving the lives of those around them—the civic reward of a confident pluralist.

But the question of what it really means to be a confident pluralist came home to me most powerfully in lessons that I learned from my father and my aunt. I grew up in a large, politically diverse family. During my youth, in one remarkable year, 1992, my aunt was on the ballot in California's Bay Area for the far-left Peace and Freedom Party, while my father was running for the US Senate from southern California as a Reagan Republican.

They would get into heated debates over our dinner table. My dad was skinny and professorial-looking, pipe smoke always curling around his head. By contrast, my aunt was a big woman with a huge belly laugh. She was gay, and she and her partner were one of the first couples to get a marriage license in San Francisco. Their debates over free markets versus public investments, and civic virtues versus experiments in living, were fierce and constant.

At first, as a young person, I found their debates confusing and disorienting. I loved and admired both. But who was right? Eventually two things became clear to me. First, they shared a common purpose: the belief that empowerment for individuals, families, and communities is the foundation of human thriving. They disagreed—often ferociously—about how to achieve it. Second, they went after ideas, not people. They never broke the bonds of love or respect, even though they vigorously disagreed.

My dad and my aunt were the first confident pluralists whom I truly got to know. Each was clear about what mattered to them and why. They practiced personal reflection. Each was ready to advance the cause of their commitment but always, as they did so, they held sacred the dignity of the human being in front of them, even in disagreement.

What Is a Confident Pluralist?

A confident pluralist is both confident in their own values and committed to the projects of pluralism and self-government for free and equal citizens through constitutional democracy. Confidence is about digging deep to understand what matters to you and why—not just holding preferences but doing the reflective work of articulating reasons for your commitments while also considering the viewpoints of others and testing their putative validity. This is the bedrock of conviction and the source of resilience in disagreement.

The point of constitutional democracy is to empower all of us to contribute to shaping our shared world—by setting our purposes in relation to each other, even when we are at cross-purposes. Pluralism follows naturally from a belief in empowerment and self-government. When people are free to chart their own courses, they will develop different visions of the good. James Madison rightly argued in *The Federalist Papers* that freedom yields diversity of thought. He argued that protection of the "diverse faculties" of humankind is "the first object of government."

That diversity then manifests at three levels:

1. **Individual**—Different people will reach different conclusions about the good life.
2. **Social**—Those individual differences give rise to diverse cultural forms.
3. **Institutional**—We must work through the institutions of constitutional democracy to empower all of us to contribute to shaping our shared world; this inevitably involves negotiating across differences, knowing that collective decisions will never perfectly match any individual's will.

This last point is the paradox of self-government: We must accept a gap between our personal preferences and collective outcomes.

Although we refer to democracy as resting on the will of the people, in fact, no single person's will ever lines up perfectly with the collective will that emerges from a process of democratic decision-making. Thanks to pluralism, the beautiful fruit of freedom, we find ourselves through our institutions involved in negotiation and compromise, the work of trying to achieve outcomes that we can broadly live with, knowing that sometimes we win and sometimes we lose. The reward for accepting this gap between our individual purposes and shared outcomes is the experience of participating in shaping our shared world.

The commitment to human flourishing through purpose, to empowerment, and to constitutional democracy as the best vehicle for empowerment brings a tough challenge with it. If we work hard to understand the good and what we personally care about so that we can steer our own lives, how on earth do we also function in a world with so many different visions of the good? How do we handle the inevitable frustration and disappointment of the democratic process? These emotions are freedom's tax. We minimize them precisely by leaning into the democratic process and participating as fully as we can, thus lodging as much of what we care about as possible in the final shared outcome. To lean into democratic practice in this way is to learn how to act as a confident pluralist, which is why confident pluralism should be lodged at the heart of civic education. How does one become this person?

Five Commitments of a Confident Pluralist

1. **Reflection**—Practices such as philosophy, theology, and literature help us examine fundamental questions—*How should I live? How should we live?* These are old Socratic questions. Developed habits of reflection are a form of attention that requires intentional cultivation. This work builds the resilience to stand firm in one's convictions under challenge and also to listen charitably.

2. **Commitment to Institutions and to Nonviolence**—Democratic institutions are not separate from us; they are the instruments of our empowerment. Protest can be important to make ourselves heard, but participation through institutions is how we gain influence and shape lasting outcomes. As Yuval Levin has argued, institutions channel conflict into constructive negotiation, making it possible to live together in freedom.
3. **Commitment to Compromise**—Compromise is not an abandonment of principle but the search for solutions that incorporate the perspectives of all affected. It's the achievement of negotiated settlements, where the clash of interests yields a fused solution that no one could have precisely anticipated in advance. No democracy can survive without compromise since, by definition, the citizenry enters into its decision-making at cross-purposes with one another and to abandon habits of compromise is to accept perpetual war at the center of social life, an unsustainable social choice.
4. **Listening Before Speaking**—In my classes, I require students to repeat back what they have heard before responding. Nine times out of ten, they have misunderstood, and the work becomes one of reaching genuine understanding before debating. This simple discipline can transform disagreements from personal clashes into genuine engagement with ideas.
5. **Protecting Human Dignity**—In a toxic culture, some will try to provoke and diminish others, holding human dignity hostage. The best response is to refuse the bait and meet hostility with generosity, or Aristotelian political friendship. This means using the practices of a friend, even when none of the emotions of friendship exist.

Among these commitments, the hardest for people to embrace are compromise and the commitment to protecting human dignity, so I will spend a bit more time on each.

The Commitment to Compromise

One challenge these days in understanding the value of compromise is that our history lessons prominently invoke the Great Compromise and the Missouri Compromise. In other words, the original compromises defining the American story are rulings that accommodated slavery. For good reason, we can no longer comfortably hold up compromises that make accommodations of that kind as shining examples of healthy democratic practice. These compromises made our nation, yet we reject them now. They cannot serve as models for the practice of democracy. We seem to be left without resources for understanding how compromise *should* operate in democratic life.

Here it can be helpful to turn to the Declaration of Independence. This text inscribed two compromises in the nation's very origin—one good, and one bad. Recovering this distinction between good and bad compromises will open up for us the possibility of taking compromise seriously as a practice we should aspire to.

Both compromises are adumbrated in the all-important second sentence of the Declaration:

> *We hold these truths to be self-evident, that all men are created equal, that they are endowed by their creator with certain unalienable rights, that among these are life, liberty, and the pursuit of happiness, that to secure these rights, governments are instituted among men, deriving their just powers from the consent of the governed, that whenever any form of government becomes destructive of these ends, it is the right of the people to alter or to abolish it, and to institute new government, laying its foundation on such principles and organizing its powers in such form as to them shall seem most likely to effect their safety and happiness.*

The good compromise lies in how the Declaration engages with the language of religion. The bad compromise lies in how it handled slavery.

On religion, the Declaration uses the words "created," "creator," "divine providence," and "supreme judge." These are polysemantic words communicating no particular doctrinal commitments. People from a variety of faiths could see themselves in this set of words. And neither were non-believers, atheists, deists, or humanists left out. In the first sentence, the Declaration names the moral foundations of its argument as being "the laws of nature and of nature's God." This phrase is something like a belt-and-suspender's phrase. If you are not a believer, then the laws of nature can explain to you what it means to say that people have natural equality as human beings, concretized in the form of citizens' rights. If you are a believer, then you will consider these moral facts as flowing from "the laws of nature's God." The combination of this phrase and the very open-ended references to a higher power constituted a compromise that gave everybody in the colonies, whether faithful or not, and regardless of which religion they adhered to, a way of affirming and connecting to the moral foundations of the text. By taking the perspectives of all affected into account, the Declaration secured a successful compromise.

The compromise on slavery stands in contrast to that, and spelling that out will require more context. The phrase "life, liberty, and the pursuit of happiness" was unusual. In the eighteenth century, the domains protected by basic rights were more commonly listed as life, liberty, and property. But by the spring of 1776, as the founders were working on drafting the Declaration, the concept of property had become closely connected to a defense of enslavement. In the fall of 1775, the British Royal Governor of Virginia, Lord Dunmore, had issued a proclamation declaring that an enslaved person who escaped and fought against the British would earn their permanent freedom. The Virginians considered this a violation of their rights of property. As the members of the

Continental Congress debated the Articles of Confederation in June and July of 1776, the question of whether enslaved people should be counted as people or property was threatening to break the joint endeavor to form a union.

The phrase "life, liberty, and property" could not be used without, in that context, signaling that the new polity, the United States of America, would in fact be committed to a defense of slavery. But people who were working on the Declaration, like John Adams and Benjamin Franklin, were already against enslavement. They didn't want such a commitment to be anchored in that document. John Adams made the argument for happiness as an alternative word. He argued for it throughout the fall of 1775 and spring of 1776. The phrase "life, liberty, and the pursuit of happiness" is an—albeit implied—anti-enslavement or abolitionist moment in the Declaration.

Indeed, Adams built on just this language in drafting the Massachusetts State Constitution in 1780. That language, inscribed in the Constitution, then became the basis for formally ending slavery in Massachusetts before the end of the Revolutionary War.

Yet just as there was an abolitionist moment in the drafting of the Declaration, there was also a pro-slavery moment. The first draft included a passage criticizing King George for violating the sacred rights of life and liberty of distant people in Africa via the slave trade. The drafters of the Declaration equally applied the vocabulary of sacred rights to themselves and to Africans. But the Continental Congress deleted that passage during its deliberations. It went too far for the Southern slave-holding interests.

In sum, the compromise in the Declaration around enslavement consisted of two rhetorical moves. First, there was the phrase invoking "life, liberty, and the pursuit of happiness" as an open-ended statement of goals and values—emphatically not a commitment to slavery but also not fully forcing the question. Second, there was the excision of the statement that would have positively affirmed the rights of people in Africa. This I consider a bad compromise. In contrast to the example around religion, this second compromise cannot be said to have the rights and interests of all who were affected by it taken into account. That's because the voices of the enslaved people played no part in the formation of that particular compromise.

This precedent gives us a clear way of characterizing the difference between good and bad compromises. A confident pluralist is somebody who, in public fora for decision-making, is ready to compromise with others by letting all voices be heard in the spirit of real viewpoint diversity. When making a good compromise, a confident pluralist will ensure that everybody who might be affected by the decision has a voice in the process. The purpose of bringing those voices together is for shared and mutual learning, to explore whether there might be an alternative path to resolution that cannot become visible *until* everyone's viewpoints and voices are heard and considered.

We cannot learn the practice of compromise unless we routinely find ourselves in the same room with people with whom we vehemently disagree.

The Commitment to Dignity

What does it mean to never let anybody hold human dignity hostage?

Too many people relate to others in a spirit of negativity, bullying, and insult. When this happens, people are taking their own human dignity hostage. They have let go of their best selves. They're also trying to take the other party's human dignity hostage. They're trying to get a rise out of them. They're trying to keep the other party from keeping their own best self front and center. Not letting other people take human dignity hostage is about responding to those moments of toxicity in a very different way than we see exhibited in the "hissy fits" on our TV screens and in the news and social media.

Two stories will clarify what I mean.

Starting in September 2015 and through 2016, I wrote several op-eds for the *Washington Post* criticizing then-candidate Donald Trump. This earned me a significant amount of incoming hate—anonymous emails and voicemails, tweets directed at me with images of nooses and gas chambers. Over a period of months, the onslaught began to affect me. It made me less willing to leave my house and spend time outdoors. I wondered which faces in the crowd might harbor such vicious hatred of me. I realized that the messages were degrading my own sense of agency. In this regard precisely, my human dignity had been taken hostage.

This situation was intolerable to me, so I asked a friend with expertise in social media archaeology to see if he could ascertain the sources. He came by my office one day to report and shared that most of the worst material was coming from countries in Northern and Eastern Europe. This appeared to be the work of a global network of right-wing agitators seeking to stir up American politics along race lines. The news caused me an exceptionally strong sense of relief. I could re-embrace my fellow Americans. I proceeded to commit myself to responding to every nasty comment I might receive in a fashion that most preserved my agency and best self. I would preserve my own dignity with every response and in so doing make space for other people's dignity to re-emerge. I would seek to sort out the real humans on the other side of those messages, from the bots and troll farms. To boil it down, I committed to responding to every message with an opening line something like, "Thank you for your kind message." While this might read as sarcasm, it's not. It's a simple expression of my best self—an openness to attending to others and a refusal to let anyone else make such a comment inappropriate.

To my great astonishment, my approach actually worked. More often than not, my interlocutor was startled out of their toxicity and came around for a reasonably respectful exchange. I'll share one example, where my interlocutor made the shift especially fast, after my first response.

> From: [XXXXXX]
> Sent: Friday, November 3, 2023 4:41 PM
> To: Allen, Danielle S. <danielleallen@fas.harvard.edu>
> Subject: Aren't you ashamed?
>
> Aren't you ashamed to be associated with an institution that supports antisemitism and terrorism? I don't know how you can sleep at night? You are a despicable human being
>
> On Nov 3, 2023, at 5:01 PM, Allen, Danielle S. <danielleallen@fas.harvard.edu> wrote:
>
> Dear Mr. -------
> Thank you for your kind note. I wonder if you've taken the time to read my own contributions on the subject? If not, you'll find them here:
> https://wapo.st/40lWdAO
>
> Best wishes,
> Danielle
>
> **From:** [XXXXXX]
> **Sent:** Friday, November 3, 2023 5:40 PM
> **To:** Allen, Danielle S. <danielleallen@fas.harvard.edu>
> **Subject:** Re: Aren't you ashamed?
>
> Dr. Allen
> Thank you for responding and sending me your writings on this subject. I found it very sensible and thoughtful and

I obviously was not well informed about your thoughts on this. These are indeed difficult times and sometimes one should spend more time thinking and taking a deep breath before lashing out at someone. Please accept my apology.

Thanks again for responding and educating me
R------

On Nov 3, 2023, at 5:58 PM, Allen, Danielle S. <danielleallen@fas.harvard.edu> wrote:

Dear R------,
Thank you very much for taking the time to read my piece, for writing back again, and for your apology. You've made my day. It is my birthday and this note is a great birthday present.
With appreciation,
Danielle

From: [XXXXXX]
Sent: Friday, November 3, 2023 6:13 PM
To: Allen, Danielle S. <danielleallen@fas.harvard.edu>
Subject: Re: Aren't you ashamed?

Dr. Allen,
Let me then wish you a very happy birthday and hope you do something very special for yourself. Even though I lashed out in hostility towards you, you turned the interaction into something very positive and taught me something about myself. (I guess that's why you're a professor;)) If only everyone could do the same thing, we'd live in a better world.

I hope at the very least I brought a little smile to your

> face on your special day. Your one of the "lights" you wrote about in your article
>
> Thanks again, Danielle, and have a very happy birthday !
> R------

The fifth commitment—protecting human dignity—may prove to be the hardest to put into action. It does not mean leaving yourself vulnerable to abuse nor seeking out exposure to abuse. It also requires calmly stating that people have crossed a line. In accepting R's apology, I was confirming that he had something to apologize for. I also have a number of security procedures in place to protect me. The commitment to human dignity requires overcoming one's own sense of being taken aback or of being attacked, and meeting toxicity with forgiveness, generosity, *and* with firmness and clarity regarding what is right.

This commitment has changed my life. It has shown me that most of us are so much better than our world currently makes us appear to be. It has rekindled my faith in the vast majority of other humans.

A Call to Action: Civic Strength Through Civic Education

The ethic of confident pluralism is deeply personal for me, with profound spiritual and psychological rewards. It enables me to move through the world always looking others in the eye, as equals. Yet this ethic is also civic. Democracy demands an ethic of confident pluralism and viewpoint diversity if a government that is of the people and also by and for the people is to thrive. Our educational institutions must cultivate in our students the habits of reflection, institution-building, compromise, engagement, and mutual respect that are rooted in the principle of viewpoint diversity and pluralism. This is equally important in K–12 institutions and in higher education. If we want a democracy capable of solving its problems, we must teach citizens not only how to argue for what they believe, but also how to debate in ways that strengthen rather than shred our bonds with one another.

The Viewpoint Diversity Paradox

by Ilana Redstone

In the aftermath of the attacks in Israel on October 7, 2023, the longstanding, but often disputed, problem of how higher education approaches contentious issues came under intense public scrutiny.[1] What we learn from this moment has profound implications not only for academic communities, but for democracy itself.

While campuses' failure to engage openly and productively with heated issues isn't new—it's often been discussed in terms of free speech, shout-downs, or self-censorship—the severity of the problem has been subject to debate[2] and sometimes even outright dismissal.[3] These shortcomings became harder to deny once university presidents resigned, students occupied buildings and built encampments, and others were afraid to walk through campus while visibly Jewish.[4]

Faced with this kind of chaos, concerned parties generally approached campus tensions the way they knew how—trying to distinguish between acceptable and unacceptable speech.[5] The focus became whether, for instance, "from the river to the sea" or "Israel is committing genocide" should be considered just another perspective or condemned as anti-Semitic.

The problem is that, as counterintuitive as it may seem, if we're trying to prepare students to participate in a robust democracy, viewpoints cannot be considered inherently acceptable or unacceptable based solely on their content—the reasoning and motivations behind them have to matter. Without considering why someone holds a particular view, we have no principled basis for making distinctions, and we end up excluding viewpoints based on the arbitrary judgments of whoever happens to be in control.

To be sure, not being able to draw lines runs headlong into the practical realities of how institutions operate. Imagine a university committee tasked with ensuring viewpoint diversity in a lecture series on racial inequality. Due to time and space constraints, the committee will have to make choices about which positions to include and which to leave out. But the committee will most likely see its charge as determining which positions are worthy of inclusion and which aren't—a fundamentally different kind of judgment than one based on practical limits. Presumably, at some point, they'll decide the series is diverse "enough," that all the "reasonable" viewpoints have been added.

As soon as we make judgments about which positions are worthy of inclusion, we're engaging in the act of categorization regarding the views that are deemed reasonable and those that aren't. Yet, we cannot achieve genuine intellectual diversity through a process that requires us to treat the acceptability of an idea as divorced from the reasoning of the person who holds it. Hence the *viewpoint diversity paradox*: Ensuring a diversity of perspectives entails value judgments, which limits the very diversity we seek to create.

Confusion on this point has allowed higher education to create and sustain a culture where an entire subset of non-progressive views on identity, fairness, equality, and harm have been automatically ruled out-of-bounds and akin to bigotry.[6] Opposition to affirmative action is racist. Denying the importance of white privilege is racist. Referring to only two sexes is transphobic. And advocating for tighter border restrictions is xenophobic.

It's a culture that has led not only to claims of censorship, but also to a deep sense of social and institutional mistrust.[7] When claims about the world—e.g., inequality is evidence of racism—take on an intrinsically moral slant, the "truth" on campuses becomes seen as both ideologically driven and compromised. Without the ability to separate disagreement from moral condemnation, political pluralism becomes impossible. That's a challenge any viewpoint diversity framework has to grapple with.

The impulse to draw lines has deep roots. Philosopher Karl Popper famously wrote in 1945, "If we extend unlimited tolerance even to those who are intolerant, if we are not prepared to defend a tolerant society against the onslaught of the intolerant, then the tolerant will be destroyed, and tolerance with them."[8] The solution, in this line of thinking, is that we have to cordon off intolerant views. What Popper *didn't* address, at least not to the best of my knowledge, is that people may have understandable or principled reasons for holding views others see as "intolerant."

The paradox of tolerance begins to collapse once we recognize that tolerance itself, as well as its limits, is not exempt from the process of democratic deliberation. Ultimately, we have a finite number of ways to manage political conflict. Potential strategies include A) compelling people to adopt a particular set of perspectives; B) separating people so they're only in contact with others with like-minded views; and C) finding ways to live together despite disagreement.

The first two options have well-known consequences. Sustaining forced compliance requires constant violence or the threat of it. It also generally leads to widespread suffering and eventual rebellion. Physical separation into ideological groups is, practically speaking, nearly impossible and will tend to lead to conflict anyway as groups end up fighting over resources and boundaries. Democracy is fundamentally about the third option, i.e. finding ways to live together *despite* deep differences, which we can't do if we're judging other people's views as bigoted.

And yet, if we don't draw lines around views we see as hateful or dangerous, what does that say about our values? After all, history has shown us that human beings are capable of terrible behavior. While a healthy democratic society can't draw lines around particular viewpoints based on their content alone, it *can* make distinctions in other ways. Take intent, for example: the *intent* to oppress, harm, or humiliate surely goes against the goal of living with differences. The problem with this, of course, is that we can rarely, if ever, know a person's true motives. Worse still, if a person truly has hateful intent, they have every reason to keep that from being known.

This creates a practical problem. If we can't reliably identify malicious motives, how can we meaningfully use intent as a criterion? A way forward lies in shifting our focus from trying to divine someone's true motivations to asking whether there are plausible non-malicious reasons someone might hold a particular position.

This approach has two advantages. First, it's epistemologically honest—it requires us to acknowledge the limits of our ability to read minds while still maintaining that intent matters. Second, it's democratically generous—we give our fellow citizens the benefit of the doubt rather than assuming the worst about their motivations. The implication of this approach is that we only exclude viewpoints when we genuinely cannot come up with legitimate reasons someone might hold them—a much higher bar than simply finding the position offensive or wrong.

This exclusion criterion turns out to be remarkably difficult to meet in practice. For instance, a person defending harsh criminal sentences might prioritize victim justice and community safety rather than cruelty. Or consider an even more counterintuitive case: Someone arguing that littering isn't inherently wrong might believe that creating jobs for cleanup crews provides economic benefits, or that nature eventually recycles all materials anyway. This doesn't make these positions correct or well-informed (although it doesn't necessarily make them wrong or ill-informed either)—it just means we can usually identify understandable human motivations behind even the most unusual perspectives. Even positions that seem morally indefensible to some often stem from recognizable human concerns.

Since legitimate reasons are discoverable for nearly any political position, an important corollary follows: Any given viewpoint could be held for either legitimate or illegitimate reasons. That someone with hateful motives would likely support a particular position doesn't mean everyone who supports that position is necessarily hateful. If we judge positions by their most explicitly hateful or obnoxious supporters, we've created a loophole that undermines our entire framework. Instead of examining whether there are plausible non-malicious reasons to hold a view, we're taking a shortcut: "Look at who else believes this—that tells us everything we need to know." This approach recreates the problem we started with because we're still determining which viewpoints are acceptable based on content, we're just doing so indirectly. We're assuming that if hateful people support something, hateful motivations must be the only reason to hold that position.

The fact that we can find legitimate reasons for nearly any position means that when we encounter views we dislike and conclude the people holding them must be immoral, there is some reasoning that we haven't fully engaged with. This suggests that the actionable solution lies in challenging and clarifying our own thinking, not in changing the thinking of the other person, an approach that's ultimately tied to the requirements of democracy itself. Democracy requires believing that most people aren't fundamentally unreasonable or malicious—and that means taking their reasoning seriously rather than assuming they need to be fixed.

This isn't just a nice sentiment—it's a practical necessity. The project of self-governance demands that everyone get an equal voice in the political process. This reflects the principle that power derives from the consent of the governed and that all citizens, regardless of status, should have an equal opportunity to influence collective decisions. It implies equal voting rights, freedom of expression, and access to the mechanisms of participation (e.g., running for office, engaging in public discourse).[9]

And yet, this commitment only makes sense if we believe that the number of people with truly odious, sadistic, or otherwise hateful motives is small—small enough that we can be confident that they, under a system of majority rule, won't gain power. If we no longer believe this to be the case, we are faced with a choice: Either maintain a commitment to equal participation and risk empowering people we see as dangerous *or* begin restricting participation to protect against those risks—thereby abandoning democracy's core principle.

Before we take up this second option, we need to ask ourselves what it means to suddenly find ourselves convinced that large numbers of our fellow citizens are ignorant or hateful. Given that democracy requires us to believe such people are few in number, one of two things must be true: Either our foundational assumption about human nature was wrong—in which case democracy was never viable in the first place—or we've made an error in judgment about our fellow citizens' reasoning and motivations. Democracy depends on our willingness to seriously consider the second possibility before concluding that the project itself is impossible.

To be sure, someone might raise the following objection: "I'm not saying *those* people shouldn't get to vote or participate in the political process—I'm just saying we need to mobilize our side to outnumber them." But when your political strategy is premised on the idea that large numbers of your fellow citizens are hateful, ignorant, or unfit to hold power, you're no longer engaged in democratic persuasion—you're engaged in a power struggle to ensure that the "reasonable" people (who happen to agree with you) maintain control.

The person making this objection might think they're being democratic by working within the system—voting, campaigning, following procedures. But they've abandoned the democratic spirit even while maintaining democratic forms. Democracy isn't just about procedures; it's about the underlying commitment to treat fellow citizens as people whose views deserve serious consideration rather than obstacles to be overcome.

By refusing to consider that you might have misjudged your fellow citizens' reasoning, you've exempted yourself from genuinely engaging with perspectives that challenge your own. And that actually makes *you* a threat to democratic discourse.

This might seem like strong language, but threats to democracy come in multiple forms. It can clearly be threatened by anti-democratic actions—like refusing to accept the results of an election or the peaceful transfer of power. But it can also be eroded by anti-democratic thinking, like the assumption that your political opponents are fundamentally unreasonable or malicious. While these threats can be separate, they often reinforce each other. Working backwards, once you know your political opponents see you as fundamentally unreasonable, it becomes easier to justify abandoning the institutions that keep empowering people who dismiss you as extremist or ignorant.

So, if hateful or malicious *intent* lets us draw lines in theory, but not in practice (because a person's true intent is invisible to an outsider), a question remains: Can we ever exclude any viewpoints from deliberation? The answer lies in democracy's foundational requirement: If implementing a viewpoint would *require* denying some people equal access to voting, running for office, participating in civic life, or enjoying the basic rights of citizenship, then we can exclude it on procedural grounds. Imagine the following distasteful argument.

> Slavery was good for the US economy. It could be good for it again. Therefore, to strengthen the economy and to reduce unemployment, making (some) people better off, we should reinstate slavery.

If we assume the speaker is being honest, his intent isn't hateful. And yet, because acting on the idea would require restricting the enslaved people's right to participate in the political process, it violates the principle we just described.

To be sure, this analysis probably feels uncomfortably detached in the context of something as morally abhorrent as slavery. Most of us share strong moral intuitions about slavery being wrong. But relying on shared moral intuitions to tell us where to draw lines creates a problem: What happens when they aren't shared? Who gets to decide which moral judgments are obvious enough to exclude viewpoints? The strength of the framework I'm suggesting lies precisely in the fact that it can exclude this idea on procedural grounds that don't depend on everyone agreeing about moral content—they only require agreement about the basic structure of democratic citizenship.

I need to make this proposed standard for exclusion one step clearer. That is, a viewpoint is only an obstacle to equal participation if implementing it *requires* giving people differential access to the political process, not simply if it *could* result in that outcome. WHY? Consider two statements about women and men:

1. "Women are less suited to leadership positions, as seen in differences in aggression and risk-taking." Such a statement could be used to argue that women should be kept from advancing to such positions, but that policy recommendation doesn't necessarily follow from the claim itself.
2. "Because women are less suited to leadership, they deserve fewer opportunities to succeed in business." Here, the claim is about using the difference to create barriers to participation.

The first statement, while I may not like it, remains eligible for democratic deliberation because believing it doesn't require advocating for unequal treatment. After all, someone could believe it while maintaining that all people deserve the same rights. The second, however, explicitly calls for denying women equal opportunities and therefore isn't eligible for democratic deliberation . The same would be true in the following example.

1. "Black Americans have lower average education levels than white Americans." While this could be used to justify unequal access to civic life, this is ultimately a descriptive claim about group differences.
2. "Because they have lower average education levels, and education is tied to making informed political choices, black votes should count less." This is a prescriptive claim calling for unequal treatment.

The key distinction here is between what a statement says versus how someone else might use it—if we exclude positions based on their potential for misuse, we're back to ruling them out of bounds based on a moral judgment rather than engaging with the reasoning behind them. To see how this distinction works in practice, let's return to the topic of Israel and Gaza and take the statement "Israel is committing genocide." We can disagree vehemently about whether the genocide statement is true or responsible, but it's difficult to argue that the only way to hold this position is with hateful intent toward Jews, i.e. it's plausible that this statement is genuinely rooted in a concern for lives lost.

Further, the actions required to stop what someone holding this view sees as genocide—such as ceasing military operations, allowing humanitarian aid, or changing military policies—wouldn't inherently require denying anyone equal participation in democratic governance. This is fundamentally different from the slavery example, where the very implementation requires treating some humans as property without political rights.[10]

Let's think through one more example. Take the statement "Trans women aren't women." While someone could arrive at this position through hostility toward trans people, there are other possible explanations too. For instance, a reasonable person could be concerned about the preservation of women-only spaces or object to the idea that gender is disconnected from any underlying biological factors. Since these concerns don't necessarily stem from hostility toward trans people, we can't assume hateful intent.

To be sure, someone could argue that the statement about trans women should be ineligible for deliberation anyway. The reasoning might be that the implications—for instance, denying them access to women's bathrooms—require treating trans women as having fewer rights than natal women. Someone might contend that this effectively creates a second-class citizenship for trans people, denying them the equal participation that democracy requires.

But this argument conflates different types of restrictions. Someone holding the view that trans women aren't actually women could still believe trans people deserve to vote, speak freely, have equal opportunities, and have equal legal standing—they could simply disagree about how sex-segregated spaces should be defined. While the line between "access to specific facilities" and "equal participation in civic life" isn't always self-evident, democratic discourse demands that the standard for exclusion remain high.

This is crucial because if we make it easy to exclude viewpoints by expanding what counts as a denial of equal participation, every policy disagreement can be drawn into question. It opens the door to the claim that, for instance, progressive tax policies would treat high earners as second-class citizens by denying them equal treatment under the law. Therefore, any discussion of progressive taxation should be ineligible for democratic—and campus—discourse.

Having established that most contentious viewpoints—even deeply uncomfortable ones—must remain eligible for democratic deliberation, a practical challenge remains. After all, campuses still need to figure out how to engage with difficult ideas productively and in a way that acknowledges people's feelings. How do we create a community and a culture that supports this? We can start by imagining a campus where the following principles form a core of the institutional culture:

> Contentious topics are morally and ethically complex. When they stop being morally and ethically complex, they generally stop being contentious. Given that, when engaging on heated and contentious topics, it's important NOT TO:
>
> - Settle for simplistic explanations or moralizing slogans implying one side is good and the other side is evil;
> - Make assumptions about other people's intent;
> - Assume that if we all had the same information we would all agree.
>
> And it's important TO:
>
> - Engage explicitly with the potential disadvantages and downsides of any position;
> - Use language precisely and acknowledge when key terms mean different things to different groups. When we use morally loaded terms, we force anyone who disagrees with us to either accept our framing or defend what has been labeled as evil and wrong.

Consider how this might play out in practice. The university committee tasked with deciding which views to include on racial inequality would no longer ask whether skepticism about systemic causes of racism constitutes a legitimate viewpoint or, rather, a harmful perspective. Instead, they'd ask whether there are plausible non-malicious reasons prompting someone to hold this view and whether it intrinsically violates the principle of equal participation. If the perspective passes both tests, it remains eligible.

It's worth noting that this approach requires a sincere commitment—it can be easy to claim a viewpoint fails one or both of the tests we've established when the real reason for exclusion is moral objection. Ultimately, the consistent application of this framework, rather than any single decision, will determine whether it succeeds.

With this in mind, an expression like "Israel is committing genocide" passes both tests. It's possible to imagine how someone could come to this position without hateful motives, and it doesn't violate our core democratic principle of equal participation. At the same time, it violates the principles for campus culture outlined above. The use of the loaded word "genocide" leaves no space to engage with potential counterarguments—such as Israel's stated security concerns or the complexities of asymmetric warfare—without appearing to condone a clear moral wrong.

Compare the initial statement to a more precise possible alternative: "I believe Israel's military response in Gaza is excessive and causing unnecessary civilian harm because . . . [specific reasoning]. However, I acknowledge Israel's security concerns and the complexities of asymmetric warfare." Using language with precision forces us to surface our underlying assumptions—whether about factual claims (does this meet the technical and legal definition of genocide?), about motivations (is Israel deliberately targeting civilians?), or about tradeoffs (should immediate humanitarian concerns outweigh long-term security considerations?). And that, in turn, creates space for genuine engagement.

The upshot is this: For too long, campuses have been asking "Which views should be allowed?" when they should be asking "How do we create environments where people can productively engage with and think through difficult ideas while maintaining a core commitment to human dignity?" For universities to move forward, they need to shift from reactive policies focused on limiting speech, constraining ideas, and responding to perceptions of offense with acquiescence to proactive approaches that build capacity for clear, precise, and open thinking. This means teaching students that contentious issues are morally complex, how to fully engage with this complexity in their thinking and in their interactions, and why intent has to matter. It also requires leaders willing to model these approaches rather than simply manage controversy.

The stakes extend far beyond campus boundaries. How universities navigate these challenges shapes not just academic discourse, but the future of democratic deliberation itself. In a world of increasing polarization, the ability to engage thoughtfully—even in the solitude and privacy of one's own mind—with a wide range of viewpoints isn't just an academic ideal. It's an essential skill for maintaining civic life.

Notes

1 Jacob Mchangama, "Free Speech Defenders Must Be Consistent," *Persuasion*, January 13, 2025, https://www.persuasion.community/p/free-speech-defenders-must-be-consistent.

2 Michael C. Behrent, "A Tale of Two Arguments about Free Speech on Campus," *Academe Magazine*, Winter 2019, https://www.aaup.org/academe/issues/105–0/tale-two-arguments-about-free-speech-campus.

3 Jeffrey Adam Sachs, "There Is No Campus Free Speech Crisis: A Close Look at the Evidence," Niskanen Center, April 27, 2018, https://www.niskanencenter.org/there-is-no-campus-free-speech-crisis-a-close-look-at-the-evidence/.

4 Stephanie Saul et al., "Penn's Leadership Resigns Amid Controversies Over Antisemitism," *New York Times*, December 9, 2023, https://www.nytimes.com/2023/12/09/us/university-of-pennsylvania-president-resigns.html.

5 Michael Herzog, "Meta's 'from the River to the Sea' Decision Legitimizes Hate Speech," *The Hill*, September 18, 2024, https://thehill.com/opinion/technology/4884240-meta-oversight-board-slogan/.

6 Harold Meyerson, "How Racist Are Republicans? Very," *The American Prospect*, October 22, 2020, https://prospect.org/blogs-and-newsletters/tap/how-racist-are-republicans-very/; "The Abbot Cancellation," MIT Free Speech Alliance, November 2021, https://mitfreespeech.org/the_abbot_cancellation_banner.php.

7 Sara Fischer, "Media Trust Hits Another Historic Low," *Axios*, October 15, 2024, https://www.axios.com/2024/10/15/media-trust-gallup-survey; Emily A. Vogels, Andrew Perrin, and Monica Anderson, "Most Americans Think Social Media Sites Censor Political Viewpoints," Pew Research Center, August 19, 2020, https://www.pewresearch.org/internet/2020/08/19/most-americans-think-social-media-sites-censor-political-viewpoints/.

8 Karl Popper, *The Open Society and Its Enemies* (London: Routledge, 1945).

9 While there are a limited number of circumstances where people can lose those rights—namely through a felony conviction or the determination of mental incapacity—these are generally viewed as exceptional cases grounded in questions of moral responsibility or cognitive ability and are not tied to political disagreement or identity. As a result, they tend to be seen as compatible with the broader democratic commitment to equal participation.

10 The Israel-Gaza example raises complex questions about how to handle positions regarding governance in other countries. For instance, if US students advocated that women shouldn't vote in other, non-democratic countries, would that be eligible for deliberation under this framework? That question is outside the scope of this chapter.

III

Viewpoint Diversity in Literature and Publishing

How Publishing Lost the Plot on Diversity

by Bernard Schweizer

During the past roughly ten years, the publishing industry has been decisively shaped by a pro-diversity paradigm. The basis of this movement is laudable: Literature and publishing have for too long been a bastion of white male privilege—thus a move toward greater diversification, both regarding the authors' own background and regarding their cast of characters and choice of themes, was long overdue. Enhancing literary diversity broadens the horizon of experiences that are represented, validated, and explored in texts. Clearly, literature makes progress in terms of viewpoint diversity when races of all shades and backgrounds, LGBTQ people, conservatives, the elderly or neurodiverse, different nationalities and cultures, etc. are featured prominently and when their backgrounds and concerns are given importance. But, as I will show in this essay, the publishing industry's practical implementation of this pro-diversity ethos has entailed a series of unintended consequences that are not only threatening creative freedom and artistic license but are also undercutting the very diversity that they were designed to foster.

Part of the problem has to do with the absence of diversity among the literary gatekeepers themselves, i.e. those ostensibly tasked with ensuring that the literary marketplace becomes a playground for more diverse voices. These gatekeepers, i.e. literary agents, editors, publishers, and reviewers, are a fairly homogenous bunch: A study in 2016 of dozens of American book publishers and review organizations found that 79 percent of the staff were white and 78 percent women.[1] If anything, the imbalance would have become even more pronounced since then. Providing a more granular approach, Alex Perez estimates[2] that 80 percent of today's literary agents are progressive, urban, middle class, white women, who tend to select a specific kind of literature to be promoted through the publishing process, i.e. narratives that appeal to their own demographic.[3] And since progressivism today is closely associated with identity politics, an ideological predisposition that thrives on essentialism and group identity, literary voices have become increasingly siloed and segregated. Under the guise of fostering diversity, therefore, today's literary gatekeepers often prescribe what themes and perspectives authors are allowed to explore and what characters or themes are off limits to them.

The most blatant way that this has played out is through the concept of "cultural appropriation," which has torpedoed imaginative freedom and caused creative tunnel vision like no other concept that mainstream publishing has recently cooked up, ostensibly in the interest of diversity and authenticity. On the surface, the ban on "cultural appropriation" is meant to safeguard cultural authenticity, proscribing superficial and stereotyped representations of identities that are not the authors' own. But the road to hell is ever paved with good intentions, and the ban on "cultural appropriation" is no exception. The chilling effects of this particular rule—which also goes under the name of "Own Voices" and "Lived Experience"—are addressed eloquently in the two essays following mine, by Henry Louis Gates Jr. and Richard North Patterson, respectively. This chapter, therefore, focuses on two less frequently cited but equally corrosive dynamics that are symptomatic for the malaise that's afflicting the world of publishing: I am referring the wolf-in-a-sheepskin role of *sensitivity readers*, who posture as protectors of diversity yet systematically subvert creative freedom and genuine viewpoint diversity; the other dynamic is the quiet erosion of viewpoint diversity caused by *ideological curation* of literary offerings, with Amazon.com taking the lead in this regard.

Sensitivity Readers

While the sensitivity reading business may not be a multi-billion-dollar industry (yet), it sure looks like a thriving cottage industry. All major publishers nowadays rely on an army of specialists tasked with tracking down, catching, and eliminating all kinds of words, ideas, idioms, perspectives, and attitudes that could give offense to any given demographic or that might fall short of a supposed gold standard of authenticity. The online marketplace Fiverr lists 190 Sensitivity Readers for hire, each one with his, her, or their own narrow specialty, ranging from "person of color sensitivity reader" and "LGBTQ sensitivity reader" to "Indian sensitivity reader" and "deaf sensitivity reader," to name just a few of the ever-proliferating menu of identity markers.[4] Beyond freelancers such as these, there are numerous agencies, large and small, that offer comprehensive sensitivity reading services, including Kevin Anderson Associates, Wicked Ink Publishing, Salt and Sage, Writing Diversely, Writing Cosmos, and a host of other sensitivity reading services. The illusion created by these services is that diversity is being served by these specialists. However, the opposite is the case, as I shall show.

To begin with, sensitivity readers are unapologetically essentialist. To pretend that one person, i.e. an individual sensitivity reader, can act as an authoritative spokesperson and judge for an entire race, culture, sexual orientation, or disability status is preposterous on the face of it. It proceeds from the simplistic presumption that entire demographics are monolithic entities which are then replicated in their entirety in each individual member of a given group. When applied to races, this is arguably an expression of racism itself. The same denial of individualism and nuance informs the assumption that all members of a supposedly "empowered" group, including artists or the poor, are uniformly conditioned to victimize members of marginalized groups. This mindset of racial and cultural homogeneity is out of touch with reality. Does a Black man from Chicago's South Side represent all of American Blackness? Does a Hispanic Miami socialite represent all Hispanic experience in America? Of course not, and neither does any sensitivity reader have the qualification to arrogate onto him or herself the right to speak on behalf an entire population, nation, race, ethnicity, or other collective formation. I wouldn't even trust a Hispanic socialite from Miami to speak for *all* Hispanic socialites of Miami.

The essentialism that undergirds the entire project of sensitivity readings is eloquently exposed in a recent book by Adam Szetela titled *That Book Is Dangerous: How Moral Panic, Social Media, and the Culture Wars are Remaking Publishing*: "In the past, Jim Crow racists came up with rules for black people. In the present, sensitivity readers come up with rules for fictional black people."[5] By locking literary characters into narrowly prescriptive, clichéd roles and imposing crude racial, gender, or other identity expectations on them, sensitivity readers are doing a disservice to the cause of diversity. The fact that these readers claim "expertise" on what constitutes identitarian authenticity by fiat, without any accreditation or validation, only exacerbates the problem. That they are doing so in order to make money casts further doubt on the moral foundation of that business: "In cases where a cisgender, heterosexual author is writing about an LGBTQ+ character, or a white author is writing about a BIPOC character, sensitivity readers are hired to manufacture the difference. They are the architects of difference."[6] In other words, to be worth their salt, sensitivity readers have to find fault with the texts they are tasked to evaluate, or they could not justify their fees.

The shortcomings of sensitivity readings do not end here: To assume that what the sensitivity reader finds "offensive" will stick in the throat of ALL members of a given demographic is, again, a baseless claim. I have taught Evelyn Waugh's arguably racist satire *Black Mischief*—at a time when it was still possible to separate author from work, and content from skill—and we had robust classroom debates around stereotypes, satirical intent, ambivalence, humor, and literary merit, but the student in the class who was most keenly interested in the book was . . . you guessed it, Black, and that wasn't because I showed unqualified enthusiasm for that novel. Still, he found it compelling and wrote a fine critical term paper on *Black Mischief*. Had a sensitivity reader deprived him of the experience of reading Waugh's unpurged novel, he'd not done my student any favor. To pretend that people of certain demographics need to be shielded from allegedly "offensive" or otherwise challenging contents is both infantilizing and condescending. To protect readers from hypothetical harm is not liable to build strength, resilience, and critical discernment—rather it is the literary equivalent of the Nanny State.

We know what happens when the literary Nanny State takes over: A big cry went up from the literary world in 2023 when Puffin Books brought out a politically correct edition of Roald Dahl's *Charlie and the Chocolate Factory*, purging the text of "offensive" words such as "fat" and "ugly," as well as "man" and "female," not to mention interpolating wholly new sentences not dreamt up by Dahl, such as this gem of inclusivity: "There are plenty of other reasons why women might wear wigs and there is certainly nothing wrong with that." What is gained by such crude bowdlerisms is a *fake appearance* of inclusiveness and diversity, in other words—*virtue signaling*. In reality, this approach is draining a work of art of its distinct voice and historical and literary identity, thereby reducing rather than enhancing the diversity of viewpoints that are made available by any given story, bringing the voice closer to a neutral tone—a regression to the mean, a literary mess of pottage.

To illustrate where this arrogant presumption of cultural

authority can lead, it is instructive to read an actual sensitivity report, as outlined in Joshua Wilson's essay "On Insensitivity."[7] The sensitivity reader of Wilson's unconventional short story, set in post-war Japan, accused the author of tentacle porn (gasp!) on the flimsy basis that the story contained the word "octopus" in a scene featuring a woman: "Women having sex with octopuses or squids," the sensitivity reader pontificated, "is one of the first things that comes up when men with little experience with Japanese women meet one." The baffled author could only assert that "my story features no nudity, sex acts, or pornography, although the word *octopus* does appear, twice." Note the sensitivity reader's astonishing certainty about what it is that ALL men with little experience of Japanese women are thinking when they meet one. The same sensitivity reader further lectured Wilson on Japanese history: "[Japan's wartime] military dictatorship ultimately was defeated by the Emperor himself, and by the regular Japanese people who listened to his counsel and sought for peace." For these and many other absurdities, the author paid a sensitivity reading agency two hundred dollars.

But that's not all: This sensitivity reader also objected to one of the characters' use of self-deprecatory language, saying

> For a white man to have a Japanese woman speak this way about a Japanese woman is to use a Japanese face as a cover for saying terrible things, in a way that is so well disguised that it may encourage other people to say similar things to other Japanese women. A narrator taking this license all too often grants similar license to readers.

This is what Pamela Paul had in mind when she called out the "illiberal scolds"[8] who now set the tone in the world of publishing. To me (and many others), the idea that imaginary characters should *not* be allowed to think deprecatory or self-deprecatory thoughts is patently absurd. As long as literature is supposed to reflect the world as it is, rife with conflict and harmony, prejudice and tolerance, compassion and hate, heroism and cowardice, we will need to put up with a certain amount of deprecatory content, simply because without it, literature would be flat and saccharine. Even fairy tales—those stories designed for children's consumption—are rife with conflict, ambiguity, violence, and occasional prejudice.

Moreover, the argument that "bad words" inevitably lead to bad outcomes cannot withstand scrutiny, either. In fact, I recommend the chapters "Words are Violence" and "Hate Speech Is Not Free Speech" in *The War on Words*[9] to read a sharp, comprehensive, and historically contextualized refutation of this outworn, flawed argument. The sensitivity reader's moral puritanism betrays a disregard for complexity and a denial of the breadth of human experience, neither of which serves the interests of authentic self-expression and diversity.

Yes, there can be bad stereotypes (as well as good ones, too), but the world will not be rid of hateful attitudes by censors who eradicate the offensive words while leaving the underlying attitudes that motivate them untouched. In fact, a good starting point for countering negative stereotypes is to hear them and then talk openly about them. Also, comically inflating stereotypes and laughing at them robs the stereotypes of their potency. Generations of Jewish comedians can testify to this, ironically employing the very antisemitic tropes that their enemies are invoking, thereby subverting their power over the mind.

Sensitivity readings like the above play havoc with the breadth, the versatility, the nuance, and the complexity of literary representations of reality. They flatten a work of art to a few aspects of its content, and they pave the way for anodyne, tamed, sanitized, and boring literature that is as harmless as a basket of lollipops (or maybe not quite as harmless, as consuming too much candy can lead to problems).

But what's the alternative? I argue that as long as we have good editors, there really is no need for sensitivity readers: If a novel is badly researched, full of embarrassing gaffes, and replete with aggressive, agenda-driven stereotypes, it doesn't take a sensitivity reader to pull the brakes on it. An intelligent, responsible editor well versed in literary history and aware of the existence of corrosive and discriminating views of vulnerable people will apply a gently corrective influence if something is truly and egregiously amiss. But a good editor can also balance potentially offensive bits of a story with the overarching aesthetic and artistic goals of the literary text and make a wholistic judgment about whether or not a story needs to be tampered with on the level of word choice, character selection, or thematic thrust, something that most sensitivity readers are incapable of doing.

Ideological Curation at Amazon.com

The other phenomenon in publishing that's ostensibly designed to improve diversity but in actual fact amounts to little more than an identitarian manipulation of the literary marketplace is the ideological curation evident at the world's largest book seller, Amazon.com. Anybody who wants to list a book for sale on Amazon.com has to provide a host of "metadata" detailing the content that customers will encounter when they look up the title on the website. Among the information that goes into the metadata are "browse categories," i.e., a set of identity markers that become associated with a book once it is offered on Amazon's website. Browse categories constitute a hierarchical, tree-like classification system that aids customers in navigating and filtering their searches, thus centrally effecting the discoverability of items on Amazon. Amazon's sales rankings are keyed to these categories. On the surface, they reflect an ordinary taxonomy of literary genres and sub-genres, but there's more to those tags than meets the eye: Indeed, browse categories also subtly reinforce a progressive identity agenda.

To place a new fiction title on Amazon, a publisher or author must choose not only a main Category and two Subcategories but also a Placement designation from a limited menu of options. It looks like this:

Category
Literature & Fiction
Subcategory
Literary Fiction
Subcategory
Select one

Placement
Literary Fiction
- [ ] Action & Adventure
- [ ] Biographical
- [ ] Black & African American
- [ ] Classics
- [ ] Contemporary
- [ ] Historical
- [ ] Humor
- [x] LGBTQ+ Literary Fiction
- [ ] Mystery, Thriller & Suspense
- [ ] Psychological
- [ ] Romance
- [ ] Sagas
- [ ] Satire
- [ ] Short Stories
- [ ] Women's Fiction

Most of the Placement designations are quite standard, such as "Biographical," "Historical," "Satire," and "Short Stories." But three of the categories stand out as oddballs in the system: "Black & African American," "LGBTQ+ Literary Fiction," and "Women's Fiction." What is going on here? Why are identity labels getting mixed up with genuine literary classifications? And why are there only THREE identity-based placement options? Why aren't "Asian American," "Native American," "Muslim American," "Hispanic," or "Jewish Fiction" on the menu?

Presumably, the purpose of such "minority" labels is to provide marginalized groups with visibility and cultural support. But if that's the case, then why is "Women's Fiction" among these choices? Anybody with a casual knowledge of the marketplace knows that the vast majority of fiction published these days is written by women, while the vast majority of novel readers are women. A spot check at my local Barnes & Noble revealed that of twenty-two titles displayed on the fiction bestseller shelf, twenty were written by women. This situation is symptomatic for the literary scene at large, and it has given rise to a whole slew of commentaries regarding the "disappearance of the literary male."[10] While statements about the "vanishing male author" may sound overly alarmist, it is true that this particular demographic has recently come in for fairly crass discrimination. In response to this, there's even a new press, Conduit Publishing, in the UK, that publishes exclusively male authors, presumably to save these voices from extinction. In this context, presenting "Women's Fiction" as if it were a marginalized or beleaguered category, commensurate with "LGBTQ+" and "Black & African American," is deeply misleading. Since women authors have 70–80 percent of the fiction market share, it would be much more accurate to regard "Men's Fiction" as an identity marker worthy of its own browse category.

But Amazon's ideologically motivated curation doesn't stop here. The arcane system of metadata configurations also requires that sellers of books combine the chosen browsing categories with a limited number of identity labels, including "women" and "men." If one combines the main category "Literature & Fiction" with the identity marker "Women" on Amazon's "metadata" template, the outcome is an ever-proliferating list of shades and nuances:

Amazon Browse Category 2
Literature & Fiction
WOMEN
Books/Literature & Fiction/Action & Adventure/**Women**'s Adventure
Books/Literature & Fiction/African American/**Women**'s Fiction
Books/Literature & Fiction/Dramas & Plays/**Women** Authors
Books/Literature & Fiction/History & Criticism/Genres & Styles/**Women**
Books/Literature & Fiction/History & Criticism/**Women** Authors
Books/Literature & Fiction/Poetry/**Women** Authors
Books/Literature & Fiction/United States/African American/**Women**'s Fiction
Books/Literature & Fiction/**Women**'s Fiction/African American
Books/Literature & Fiction/**Women**'s Fiction/Contemporary **Women**
Amazon Browse Category 3

The list of variations is so long, one has to scroll far down to reach the bottom.

But if one combines the main category, "Literature & Fiction" with "Men," the result is ONE SINGLE DESIGNATION, i.e. "Men's Adventure." Are men such benighted creatures that only the promise of adventure will prompt them to pick up a novel?

One might shrug this off, thinking *So what?* But the thing is, Amazon's eccentric taxonomy has real-world consequences. If a person entered a brick-and-mortar bookstore looking for a

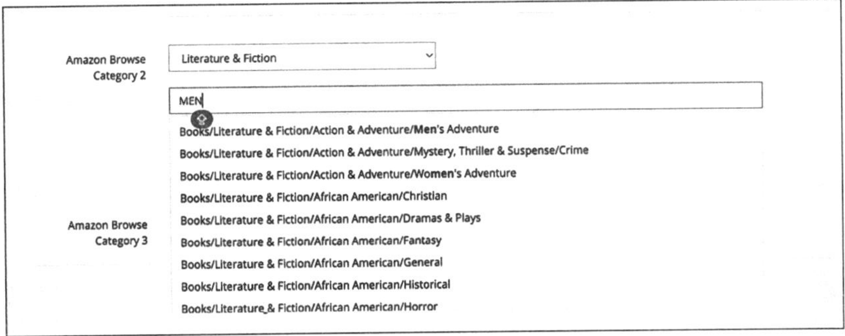

gritty, male-authored novel written in a—let's say—Cormac McCarthy vibe, and if that person ended up wandering aisle after aisle labeled "Women's Fiction," "Women's Adventure Fiction," "African American Women's Fiction," "Women's Dramas and Plays," "Women's Poetry," etc., we could not fault said customer for leaving the store empty-handed. But that's pretty much what the browsing experience on Amazon's website is like. The curation model is calibrated to disfavor works written by men as well as works aimed specifically at male readers. This is not the best way to promote a diverse readership.

It's not just that there are no (digital) bookshelves and browse categories on Amazon.com that welcome the male reading public. Other subpopulations are likewise neglected. What about literary classifications that acknowledge elderly, conservative, libertarian, working class, anarchist, atheist, humanist, autistic, bipolar, neurodivergent, Mormon, Asian American, Native American, Muslim American, Hispanic, Jewish, or Hindu readers? Don't they deserve their own "Placement Categories"? Better yet, let's get rid of identity tags altogether and instead celebrate sheer artistic excellence. As the literary critic Dennis Scheck put it: "The point of literature is not to confirm or reinforce our identity. Literature gives us the freedom to leave our identity."

In conclusion, the efforts of sensitivity readers and of ideological curators alike are not only ineffectual when it comes to promoting diversity of viewpoints in the literary marketplace, they are actually counterproductive, giving rise to new inequities, preferences, and distortions. Instead of approaching the question of diversity with a quota mindset—attempting to socially engineer the field of literary production while (implicitly) legislating the flow of ideas—it is more promising to throw the doors open to all comers and then apply rigorous literary and aesthetic standards when it comes to selecting the "winners" in the contest for shelf-space, the public attention, and a publisher's budget for new voices. Amazon's efforts at bolstering under-represented voices merely exchanges one set of preferences for another, while shadow-banning whole demographics that are not the beneficiaries of this ideological tendency. Rather than augmenting diversity, Amazon invests in promoting a category of writing (women's fiction) that is already dominating the market. As for sensitivity readers, rather than serving the goal of diversity, they introduce a new identity separatism that denies the common humanity of writers and readers alike while throwing up barriers to the imagination and censoring both minority and majority writers. But, as the following essay by Richard North Patterson clearly demonstrates, diversity and censorship are never to be reconciled, and a principled stance on anti-censorship is the best guarantee to ensure diversity of viewpoints.

Notes

1 "Publishing industry is overwhelmingly white and female, US study finds," *The Guardian*, January 27, 2016, https://www.theguardian.com/books/2016/jan/27/us-study-finds-publishing-is-overwhelmingly-white-and-female.

2 Alex Perez, "All the sad white literary ladies" *Compact Magazine*, December 22, 2022, https://www.compactmag.com/article/all-the-sad-white-literary-ladies/.

3 See also "Women now dominate the book business. Why there and not other creative industries?" on *Planet Money*, NPR, April 4, 2023, https://www.npr.org/sections/money/2023/04/04/1164109676/women-now-dominate-the-book-business-why-there-and-not-other-creative-industries; For a nuanced case study of the gender imbalance in publishing, read

Michael Mohr's Substack titled "Are Women Preventing Men from Publishing Novels?," May 20, 2025, https://michaelmohr.substack.com/p/are-women-preventing-men-from-publishing.

4 For more information on these sensitivity readers: https://www.fiverr.com/gigs/sensitivity-reader.

5 Adam Szetela, *That Book Is Dangerous: How Moral Panic, Social Media, and the Culture Wars are Remaking Publishing* (MIT Press, 2025), 24.

6 Szetela, *That Book Is Dangerous*, 27.

7 *Heresy Press Newsletter* #14: https://heresy-press.com/heresy-press-newsletter-14/#guest.

8 Pamela Paul, "There's more than one way to ban a book," *New York Times*, July 24, 2022, https://www.nytimes.com/2022/07/24/opinion/book-banning-censorship.html.

9 *The War on Words: 10 Arguments Against Free Speech—And Why They Fail*, by Greg Lukianoff and Nadine Strossen (Heresy Press, 2025).

10 Among the recent examples are "Why Did the Novel Reading Man Disappear" by Joseph Bernstein, *New York Times*, July 3, 2025; "The Vanishing White Male Writer" by Jacob Savage, *Compact*, March 21, 2025; "The Disappearance of Literary Men Should Worry Everyone" by David J. Morris, *New York Times*, Dec. 7 2024; "Vanishing Male Writers: What the Data Shows" by Michael Mohr, Substack, May 17, 2025; "The Disappearance of Male Authors" by David Greenfield, Substack, December 15, 2024; "Where have all the young male novelists gone?" by Barry Pierce, *Dazed*, November 23, 2021; "From Misogyny to No-Man's Land: The vanishing male in contemporary literature" by Ross Barkan, Substack, May 11, 2024.

The Suffocating Censoriousness of Identity Authorship

by Richard North Patterson

(Originally published on Substack, July 28, 2023)

In a recent essay written for the *Wall Street Journal*, I detailed the experience of having numerous American publishers reject my latest work of fiction after publishing twenty-two prior novels, sixteen of them *New York Times* bestsellers. But what transcends the fate of this particular book is the predominant reason for this resistance: that as a white author, I should not have presumed to pen a work of imagination which featured Black characters grappling with my country's ongoing racial problems.

Happily, I found an independent publisher willing to publish *Trial*. But the larger issue is what my experience says about the toxicity of preemptive censorship based on the race of the author.

A bit of background. I am also a political commentator. In writing over three hundred columns or essays between 2015 and 2021, I was struck by how many were suffused by our tribulations of race—including discriminatory law enforcement; the systematic efforts of Republicans in states like Georgia to prevent Blacks from voting; the mass exploitation of racial anger and anxiety by right-wing politicians and media; the rise of white nationalism; and the difficulty of obtaining a fair trial for Black defendants in racially-charged cases.

I also believe in the power of a good story to engage a wider audience with pressing social problems. As my late friend Pat Conroy once remarked, "Fiction is where I go to tell the truth." So, I conceived a narrative culminating in the televised trial of an eighteen-year-old Black voting rights worker for capital murder, stemming from the fatal shooting of a white sheriff's deputy after a late night traffic stop in rural Georgia.

Obviously, I could not write this novel responsibly without doing the work required to ground fiction in reality—including interviewing people where they lived about their actual experience of my chosen subject. So, I traveled to a county in southwest Georgia with a harsh racial past and divisive present.

My interviewees included numerous Blacks immersed in the struggle for voting rights: judges, law enforcement officers, ministers, civil rights and defense attorneys, politicians, community leaders, voting rights activists, elected officials, and ordinary citizens. Fortunately, these Georgians were uniformly generous in sharing with me their own challenges, helping to shape my narrative while immeasurably enriching my fictional characters.

The result was a manuscript which my agents believed equaled my strongest and most commercially successful work. But they also worried that this book would fall prey to the new theology in American publishing: that only a Black author is entitled to write fiction which includes the perspective of Black characters, particularly with respect to problems of race which—while they should concern us all—directly impact Blacks.

Their misgivings proved prophetic. None of the publishers who rejected my book suggested that it was in any way racially insensitive or obtuse. Rather, the principal problem was my identity: the insistence that only a Black author with the "lived experience" of racism could safely write fiction focused on racial discrimination.

But the core question has nothing to do with me in particular. Rather, it applies to anyone who dares to write fiction: Should empathy and imagination be allowed to cross the lines of racial identity?

To me, this goes not only to the nature of literature, but to the quality of our society at large. For to repress books based on authorial identity is destructive to the essence of creativity and inimical to the spirit of a pluralist democracy.

To begin, in literary terms, this newly–minted dispensation is profoundly anti-historical. Over the last three centuries a particularly rich vein of fiction has been novels of social realism by authors like Emile Zola and Charles Dickens, explicitly intended to awaken readers to the privation, and often the perspective, of working-class people. Nor did such Americans as Mark Twain, Frank Norris, Upton Sinclair, John Steinbeck, and Tom Wolfe shrink from examining race or class.

These novelists were white men of their time who, nonetheless, believed that fiction could address important subjects beyond the prism of authorial identity. Accordingly, their novels were distinguished by assiduous research into experiences outside their own. Not only did these books enrich the broader stream of literature; they deepened the understanding of readers about societal problems they might not have otherwise considered, including the lives of those who confronted them.

Each of these authors chose to transcend their own origins. Can one seriously argue that Western literature would be better off had they confined their ambitions to the suffocating cul-de-sac of identity authorship defined by race or class, denying generations of readers the absorption and enlightenment offered by *David Copperfield* or *Huckleberry Finn* or *The Octopus* or *The Jungle* or *The Grapes of Wrath* or *Bonfire of the Vanities*? If so, there goes *Othello*. Or, whatever its flaws, the modern American classic *To Kill a Mockingbird*. But the larger point is this: Assuming that authors can have no insight beyond their own ethnicity, but universal comprehension within it, is preposterous as a template for writing fiction.

To embrace such a primitive doctrine of ethnic determinism necessitates a level of analysis so oblivious—not least to the infinite varieties and limitations of human experience within our (frequently arbitrary) racial categories—as to be risible. Race, by itself, is no guarantor of authenticity. Imagine, if you will, the patrician Wall Street lawyer Louis Auchincloss as the intuitively gifted chronicler of impoverished whites in Appalachia. Or the aristocratic Anthony Powell deciding that his whiteness equipped him to write four novels of working-class Britain instead of the elegant volumes about privileged Brits comprising *A Dance to the Music of Time*. But even taken at face value, choosing an author's racial identity as a basis for preemptive censorship ignores every other component of good fiction: narrative, characterization, dialogue, descriptive power, a sense of place, richness of language, psychological acuity, curiosity about others and, as necessary, assiduous research. Most of all, it obliterates the essential engine of literature and, indeed, of compassion : the capacity to imagine, and to empathize with, lives different than our own.

By redlining literature into ethnic neighborhoods, the proponents of creative segregation elevate race above all other factors which separate one human being from another. In truth, to write about any character whatsoever is, inevitably, to step outside ourselves in order to embrace viewpoints different from our own. Whatever our origin, we are each the product of infinite variables—not only ethnicity, but heredity, family, environment, social class, opportunities, mischances, the predominance in our lives of love or trauma. Indeed, in our own "lived reality" we spend every day of our actual lives trying to understand "the other"—people who, regardless of race, are so different from us that they defy easy understanding.

But the crabbed logic of identity authorship suggests that it is impossible for any single author to write fiction which reflects the diversity of America. Imagine, for example, a book centered on a white man and a Black woman. Must it be written by co-authors, one white and one Black? Or, to ensure "authenticity of voice" must they be a Black woman and a white man? Must a novel whose characters reflect our panoramic diversity of race and background be written by multiracial committee, lest it be preemptively censored? Or, instead of imposing censorship arbitrarily rooted in identity, should we continue to entrust fiction to the informed imagination of writers, and the collective judgment of readers left free to read what they choose?

In saying this, I don't minimize for a moment the importance of race in dividing the lived reality of whites from that of Blacks, or the ongoing role of racism in the warp and woof of American society. That's why I wrote the book. Any author who presumes to write outside their racial identity assumes the responsibility for undertaking whatever work serves as a prerequisite to doing it well—or refrain from doing it at all. But it serves no one to elevate a presumption of incapacity—or capacity—based on race into a license for censorship.

Soon enough, this imaginative straitjacket can reduce writers of fiction to representatives of a personal experience rigidly defined by race. If white authors are barred from addressing America's toils of race, Black authors will be effectively conscripted as the sole chroniclers of a profound social malady which is rightly the responsibility of every American. In a curious way, the idea that it is notionally impossible for white authors and, by extension, whites in general to comprehend the effects of racism on their Black fellow citizens can have a pernicious side effect: relieving whites of the responsibility to try.

Indeed, one of the telling byproducts of my own experience has been the reaction to it by prominent Black intellectuals. Asked for comment by the *Boston Globe*, the distinguished literary scholar, author, and Harvard professor Henry Louis Gates, a longtime advocate of the freedom to write, responded: "Art has to be open to everyone. The act of imagination cannot be censored. We simply cannot allow anyone to stand at the gate holding signs that say, 'Whites Only' or 'Blacks Only,' or in this case,

'No Whites Allowed.' We have done our best to dismantle the perverse logic of Jim Crow, characterized by the fallacious concept of 'separate but equal.' We must never allow any form of Jim Crow to be transposed onto the world of literature and art."

Similarly, Professor Tyler Austin Harper of Bates College defended the primacy of imagination: "In the view of racial solipsists, it is deemed illegitimate—inappropriate and even appropriative—to assume that it is possible to understand the lived experience of another. . . . And in a trivial sense, of course, this is obviously correct. I will never 'truly understand' what is it like to be a disabled woman, or a Ukrainian immigrant, or a tax-avoiding billionaire. But there is a difference between drawing limits to what we can reasonably know about others and asserting that we should all stay trapped in prisons of our own positionality, unable to reason about—or simply imagine—being other than ourselves."

Indeed, my own observation suggests that censorship based on the race of the author is primarily a project driven by white people who embrace a perversely proscriptive mutation of racial progressivism, rooted in a combination of condescension with ideological authoritarianism and a blinkered view of humanity. Concerning his own scholarship, Professor Harper writes of a parallel experience in academia: "Over the last decade, I have been persistently dumbfounded by comfortable white (supposedly 'woke') faculty members suggesting that a Black person isn't sufficiently focused on their own Blackness. With a single exception, every time I've been criticized for studying white authors, it was a progressive-presenting white academic levying the complaint."

So, too, with publishing. Viewed in this light, the self–righteousness inherent in enforcing the preemptive censorship of fiction based on authorial identity is redolent with irony. Given the demographics of the major publishing houses in Manhattan, it is near-certain that a great majority of publishers who objected to my identity are white and have little or no experience of the challenges facing the Black Georgians who spoke to me from their own hard experience. For these publishers to imagine themselves the literary benefactors of Black America bespeaks a self-flattering and lamentably unexamined paternalism. Do they never look in the mirror and see reflected the book banners and racial history suppressors of the right?

Nor, it seems, have they reflected on the nature of publishing—or literature itself. Authors aren't like applicants competing for the same job. Nor is fiction fungible. Each novel is its own creation, unique to its author; it exists only because that author imagined it. If a particular author is allowed to publish a meritorious book, it hardly means that a different novel by some presumptively more suitable author will not be published. Publishing is not a zero-sum game.

To the contrary, a regime of preemptive censorship means that there will be fewer good books to read—including those which are never written for fear of cancellation. Indeed, preemptive censorship is particularly insidious because it is largely invisible, occurring behind closed doors of publishing houses rather than subject to public debate or, equally, in self-censorship which prevents books from being written at all. As I noted in the *Wall Street Journal*: "Consider the plight of a gifted young writer driven to base a first novel in an identity different from their own—a novel that might then be quashed along with the potential for a literary career. How badly will their chances of publication be diminished depending on their identity? What chances will they decide not to take in order to keep on writing? And how would the rest of us know that our potential reading was the poorer for it?"

Enough. We don't need a race–based limitation on citizenship in the world of letters premised on the insistence that it is impossible, even arrogant, to deploy authorial imagination beyond one's racial identity. Instead, we need a capacious literary sensibility that unshackles the creative gifts of diverse fiction writers who make a conscientious commitment to cast off the myopia of tribe. Literature should expand our humanity, not shrink it.

Literary Freedom Is an Essential Human Right

by Henry Louis Gates Jr.

(Originally published in the *New York Times*, October 12, 2021)

"The freedom to write": PEN America's always resonant motto has a special resonance for Black authors, because for so many of them, that freedom was one they fought hard for. "Liberation" and "literacy" were inextricable. "For the horrors of the American Negro's life there has been almost no language," as James Baldwin once noted. Recall, first, that in many states it was illegal for an enslaved person even to learn how to read and how to write. Then the barbarities of the slave trade, the Middle Passage, and cradle-to-grave bondage were followed by another century of lynching, Jim Crow segregation, disenfranchisement, and officially sanctioned forms of violence. Does the English language fail us, Baldwin wonders, in the face of racist terror? No, he decides; we must embrace it, occupy it, refashion it in our images, speak it in our own voices. We must deploy it to redress this terror. "To accept one's past—one's history," as Baldwin insisted, "is not the same as drowning with it; it is learning how to use it." This, surely, is integral to the freedom to write—the freedom to bear witness to the full range of our common humanity, and all that that entails, no matter how uncomfortable the process can be.

And what of the freedom to learn? Who has the right to study, the right to teach, to broach fraught subjects at a time when the temptation to police culture has never been higher? Today, partisans in various states are passing laws and resolutions in order to regulate what teachers can say, aiming to exclude critical race theory, the *New York Times*'s 1619 Project, and even ban words such as "multiculturalism," "equity" and "whiteness." But we must not exempt ourselves from scrutiny; whenever we treat an identity as something to be fenced off from those of another identity, we sell short the human imagination.

I'm moved that this award is being presented by two people quite dear to me, one a former professor, Wole Soyinka, who introduced me to the highest reaches of the mythopoetic imagination, and the other a former student, Jodie Foster, whose own early work on Toni Morrison was so brilliantly insightful. Together, they represent ideals of education I hold sacred. The idea that you have to look like the subject to master the subject was a prejudice that our forebears—women seeking to write about men, Black people seeking to write about white people—were forced to challenge. In the same year that Rosa Parks refused to move from the white section of that public bus, Toni Morrison completed a master's thesis at Cornell on Virginia Woolf and William Faulkner, taking a seat in the white section of the modernist canon. Any teacher, any student, any reader, any writer, sufficiently attentive and motivated, must be able to engage freely with subjects of their choice. That is not only the essence of learning; it's the essence of being human.

The great Soyinka helped me grasp this when I came to study with him at the University of Cambridge almost five decades ago. Despite the fact that I wasn't African, let alone Yoruba, Wole welcomed me into his mythical, metaphysical world, dense with the metaphor, potency, and portent of an alien set of divinities.

And what exhilaration I felt, exploring these new realms. From my churchgoing youth in West Virginia, I was put in mind of a passage from the Book of Jeremiah: "Call unto me, and I will answer thee, and show thee great and mighty things, which thou knowest not!"

But then Black Africa's first Nobel laureate in literature had himself studied Shakespeare with the great English critic G. Wilson Knight, who later hailed him as among his most remarkable students. The literary imagination summons us all to dwell above what W. E. B. Du Bois called "the veil" of the color line. As he wrote, yearningly: "I summon Aristotle and Aurelius and what soul I will, and they come all graciously with no scorn or condescension. So, wed with Truth, I dwell above the veil." Du Bois never let anyone tell him to stay in his lane. When he needed to, he paved his own. As a lifelong dissident, he also knew that liberation was not secured by filtering out dissident voices; courage, not comfort, was his ideal.

What I owe to my teachers—and to my students—is a shared sense of wonder and awe as we contemplate works of the human imagination across space and time, works created by people who don't look like us and who, in so many cases, would be astonished that we know their work and their names. Social identities can connect us in multiple and overlapping ways; they are not protected but betrayed when we turn them into silos with sentries. The freedom to write can thrive only if we protect the freedom to read—and to learn. And perhaps the first thing to learn, in these storm-battered days, is that we could all do with more humility, and more humanity.

Contributors

Nafees Alam is an associate professor of social work at the University of Nebraska, senior director of policy and research at the Institute for Liberal Values, and senior scholar at ProSocial Workers, known for research and commentary on viewpoint and political diversity in social work.

Danielle S. Allen is James Bryant Conant University Professor of Political Philosophy and Ethics at Harvard University, author of *Our Declaration: A Reading of the Declaration of Independence in Defense of Equality*, and a leading scholar of democracy and citizenship.

Mark Bauerlein is Professor Emeritus of English at Emory University and a senior editor at *First Things*, known for cultural commentary and author of *The Dumbest Generation: How the Digital Age Stupefies Young Americans and Jeopardizes Our Future.*
Komi Frey is a visiting scholar at the University of Pennsylvania and former Director of Faculty Outreach at the Foundation for Individual Rights and Expression (FIRE), known for research and commentary on academic freedom and higher education policy.

Henry Louis Gates, Jr. is the Alphonse Fletcher University Professor and Director of the Hutchins Center for African & African American Research at Harvard University. An Emmy Award-winning filmmaker, he hosts the genealogy series *Finding Your Roots* on PBS and is the author of many books, including, most recently, *The Black Box: Writing the Race*.

Jonathan Haidt is a social psychologist and Professor of Ethical Leadership at NYU's Stern School of Business. He is the author of three New York Times best sellers: *The Righteous Mind* (on morality and politics), *The Coddling of the American Mind* (with Greg Lukianoff, on universities and Gen Z), and most recently, *The Anxious Generation* (on youth mental health).

Keith J. Hand is a Professor of Law at the University of California College of the Law, San Francisco, where he focuses on Chinese legal reform and viewpoint diversity in legal education. He is the author of *Resolving Constitutional Disputes in Contemporary China.*

John Inazu is the Sally D. Danforth Distinguished Professor of Law and Religion at Washington University in St. Louis, author of *Confident Pluralism: Surviving and Thriving Through Deep Difference*, and a scholar of First Amendment freedoms and pluralism.

Yascha Mounk is a GermanAmerican political scientist and Professor of the Practice of International Affairs at Johns Hopkins University, author of *The Identity Trap: A Story of Ideas and Power in Our Time*, and moderator of the podcast *The Good Fight.*

Rollie Olson is Research & Media Manager at Interfaith America, writing on pluralism, civic life, and democratic engagement.
Eboo Patel is the Founder and President of Interfaith America, the nation's premier interfaith organization. As a civic leader, speaker, and author of five books including *We Need to Build: Field Notes for Diverse Democracy*, his work advances pluralism and interfaith cooperation.

Richard North Patterson is a political commentator, columnist, and former trial lawyer, as well as a *New York Times* bestselling author of acclaimed legal and political novels such as *Conviction, Balance of Power,* and, most recently, *Trial.* His fiction explores justice, politics, and societal conflict.

Ilana Redstone is an associate professor of sociology at the University of Illinois at Urbana-Champaign, author of *The Certainty Trap: Why We Need to Question Ourselves More — and How We Can Judge Others Less*, and a scholar of social dynamics and polarization.

Hollis Robbins is a Professor of English and Special Advisor for Humanities at the University of Utah, author of *Forms of Contention: Influence and the African American Sonnet Tradition*, as well as a noted scholar of African American literature and cultural history.

Bernard Schweizer is a literary scholar with a long list of publications and Professor Emeritus at Long Island University. He founded Heresy Press in 2023 as a haven for outspoken fiction and unfettered ideas.

Jesse Singal is an American journalist and contributing writer known for social-science commentary and the co-host of the podcast *Blocked and Reported*. He authored *The Quick Fix: Why Fad Psychology Can't Cure Our Social Ills*.

Bret Stephens is a Pulitzer Prize–winning columnist for *The New York Times*, known for his commentary on foreign policy, politics, and culture, and for his independent perspective. He is the founding editor of Sapir, a quarterly journal of Jewish thought.

Nadine Strossen is a New York Law School Professor Emerita, a past president of the American Civil Liberties Union (1991-2008), and a Senior Fellow with FIRE. Her most recent book is *The War On Words: 10 Arguments Against Free Speech—And Why They Fail*, co-authored with Greg Lukianoff.

John Tomasi is a political philosopher and Professor of Political Science at Brown University, the inaugural President of Heterodox

Academy, and author of *Free Market Fairness* and *Liberalism Beyond Justice*. He focuses on integrating market liberty with social justice, promoting viewpoint diversity, and advancing open inquiry in higher education.

Tyler J. VanderWeele is the John L. Loeb and Frances Lehman Loeb Professor of Epidemiology at Harvard T.H. Chan School of Public Health, director of the Human Flourishing Program, and author of *Explanation in Causal Inference*.

Jonathan Zimmerman is the Judy & Howard Berkowitz Professor of Education and History at the University of Pennsylvania and author of *The Amateur Hour: A History of College Teaching in America* and other books on education and culture.

Other Heresy Press Titles

Fiction:

Nothing Sacred: Outspoken Voices in Contemporary Fiction edited by Bernard Schweizer and James Morrow

Deadpan by Richard Walter

Animal by Alan Fishbone

Unsettled States by Tom Casey

Devil Take It by Daniel Debs Nossiter

Alice, or The Wild Girl by Michael R. Liska

The Hermit by Katerina Grishakova

Tomorrow, the War by Max Watman

Nonfiction:

The War on Words: 10Arguments Against Free Speech—And Why They Fail by Greg Lukianoff and Nadine Strossen

Half-Jew—Full Life: The Unlikely Journey of a Voluntary Jew from Nazi Persecution to the American Dream by Georgette Bennett

Mission Statement

Heresy Press Promotes freedom, honesty, openness, dissent, and real diversity in all of its manifestations. We discourage authors from descending into self-censorship, we don't blink at alleged acts of cultural appropriation, and we won't pander to the presumed sensitivities of hypothetical readers. We also don't judge works based on the author's age, gender identity, racial affiliation, political orientation, culture, religion, non-religion, or cancellation status. Heresy Press's ultimate commitment is to enduring quality standards, i.e., literary merit, originality, relevance, courage, humor, and aesthetic appeal.

Newsletter

Don't miss the Heresy Press Newsletter:
https://heresy-press.com/newsletter